Empowering Young Christians:

Developing Bible-Based Leadership and Soft Skills

Cary J. Green, PhD

First published by Dog Ear Publishing
4011 Vincennes Rd
Indianapolis, IN 46268
www.dogearpublishing.net

dog ear
PUBLISHING

ISBN: 978-1-4575-4099-8

This book is printed on acid-free paper.

Printed in the United States of America

Contents

Acknowledgments

I thank the staff at Dog Ear Publishing for their efforts to make this book a reality. I also thank Christina Guthrie for her excellent editorial input. Her effort greatly improved my book.

I also thank the many reviewers whose input enhanced the content of my book.

I gratefully acknowledge the Lockman Foundation for allowing me to use the New American Standard Bible® for my Scripture quotations.

Dedication

To my Savior, Jesus Christ.

And to Nell and Reshma.

Introduction

Do you want to learn key skills that help you succeed in high school and college? Would you like to learn skills employers seek and that will prepare you for a productive, rewarding career? Are you interested in improving your leadership ability? Do you want a deeper relationship with Jesus Christ? Do you want to live the abundant and successful life that God has planned for you? If so, this book is for you.

One of the most important things to understand when you are young is that intelligence alone won't make you successful. You must develop leadership and soft skills. **Leadership is the ability to influence others, and *soft skills* are a collection of abilities, behaviors, and attitudes that increase your effectiveness.** Many young people struggle unnecessarily and fail to fully develop these key skills because they do not truly understand their importance. Furthermore, many young people "don't know that they don't know" the importance of these skills.

In this book, you discover leadership and soft skills within a framework of the 3Rs: **Readiness**, **Relationships**, and **Results**. **Readiness** teaches you self-awareness and emphasizes the need to understand yourself, develop a positive attitude, look for and take advantage of opportunities, and overcome challenges. **Relationships** teaches you to communicate effectively, forge authentic connections in your personal and professional life, and to be professional. **Results** teaches you to be future-oriented and emphasizes the need to know your values and priorities, set and achieve goals, solve problems, and to be accountable. In other words, **Readiness** focuses on you, **Relationships** focuses on your interactions with others, and **Results** focuses on your ability get the job done.

As a Christian, you must embrace God's plan for your life and allow Him to work in and through you. Many young Christians don't seek God's plan for their lives, and they do not tap into God's great power. As a result, many Christians fail to experience the abundant and successful life God has for them. Throughout this book, you discover scriptural references and Biblical principles for developing leadership and soft skills. By following these scriptural references and Biblical principles, you can deepen your relationship with Jesus Christ, enhance your development of leadership and soft skills, and experience the abundant and successful life God has planned for you.

This book contains practical advice and hands-on exercises to help you apply what you are learning. You will learn to seek God's guidance and to look for opportunities to enhance your leadership and soft-skills development.

By learning and applying leadership and soft skills, you will set yourself apart from your peers and increase your likelihood of success when applying for college, scholarships, internships, awards, and jobs. You will possess skills that empower your success in your education.

Furthermore, soft skills empower your career success. I interact with employers and career counselors, and I often ask them how I can better prepare young people for successful careers. A very common answer is that young people need to improve their soft skills. Indeed, a quick Internet search of "soft skills" yields numerous articles describing the need for, and general lack of, these skills in recent college graduates.

For example, to succeed as an engineer, you obviously must understand engineering. However, you also must use soft skills such as communication, collaboration, and professionalism to work effectively with your clients and coworkers. Soft skills are not tied to any particular career or discipline and are sometimes called "transferable skills" because you can transfer these skills to different careers. By developing soft skills as a student, you can improve your performance in school, and you can then transfer these skills to your career.

Leadership skills are also important. The greater your leadership ability, the greater is your ability to leverage the skills and abilities of others. As an effective leader, you can accomplish much more through the people you lead than you can by yourself. You must develop your leadership skills if you want to influence others and truly make a difference in your family, school, community, workplace, and world. Remember that leadership is the ability to influence people and is not dependent on your title. You may be in a leadership role now. Finally, many of the skills that help in your education and career also enhance your personal life. Indeed, the ability to communicate is valuable in all aspects of your life. Knowing how to listen effectively and how to have a difficult conversation can come in handy when talking with family and friends.

How Do You Develop Your Leadership and Soft Skills?

To improve at anything, you must know what you need to know, develop the abilities and behaviors you need, and have the right attitude. In this book, I will show you much of what you need to know. Through Scripture, exercises, examples, and mentoring activities, you can develop and apply the abilities and behaviors you need. Although I can provide information and give you opportunities to grow, the choice of attitude and effort ultimately is yours. If you are willing, we can begin a journey together to develop your leadership and soft skills.

Perhaps you doubt your potential to grow as a leader or develop soft skills. Don't let a lack of confidence or prior failures hold you back. **Call on God's strength, put forth effort, apply the concepts in this book, and you will grow as a Christian and as a leader.** I know several successful people who have overcome setbacks or others telling them that they would not succeed. And later in this book, I will share a personal example of overcoming a setback that had caused me to doubt my abilities and nearly drop out of college.

How Can You Get the Most Out of This Book?

To fully realize the benefits of this book, apply what you learn. You must have the goal to improve and work deliberately to improve your performance through practice. If you want to improve your three-point shooting ability, you can't just read a book on basketball—you have to shoot a lot of three-pointers. Developing your soft skills and leadership ability is similar; you must purposefully work to develop those skills.

I suggest you read this book in its entirety to get the "big picture." Read each scriptural reference carefully. Ask God to help you develop the skills you need for success. Pray for God to reveal His plan for your life, and let Him guide you.

Keep a journal of the thoughts, questions, and ideas that come to mind. After you have read the whole book, read it again, answering the questions and working the exercises within and at the end of each chapter. Review the summary at the end of each chapter. Review again any material that is not clear. Be sure that you really understand the material in each chapter rather than just check it off as having been read.

As you grow, you will find your context changes, and you may seek growth in different areas; ask God to reveal areas to focus on. By re-reading and working through this book on a regular basis, you will be on the path to continual progress. Pick a time such as your birthday, beginning of the school year, or some other meaningful time and commit to reading this book again. How will you know when to stop? That's easy. You can stop when you no longer find areas to work on.

Make a commitment to grow and realize that developing leadership and soft skills is a process. Seek a mentor to hold you accountable and to help you on your journey. You might ask a counselor, teacher, boss, coach, or pastor to be your mentor. You also might ask a leader in your community.

Christians are Divinely Empowered to Succeed

Your success is the ultimate goal of this book, and your success requires leadership and soft skills. More importantly, your success requires you to trust God to work in and through your life. You achieve true success when you live according to God's plan, accomplish what He calls you to do, and when you receive the blessings He has for you.

God empowers Christians to develop leadership and soft skills and to live the abundant and successful life He has planned for them. To be a Christian, you must accept Jesus Christ as your personal Lord and Savior. To truly experience the abundant and successful life that God has for you, embrace God's plan for your life, obey Him, and stay faithful.

Receive Salvation

If you have not already done so, your highest priority is to confess that you are a sinner and accept Jesus Christ as your Lord and Savior. You may ask, "What's the big deal about confessing that I am a sinner?" The big deal is that God loves you more than you can comprehend, and He desires to spend eternity with you in Heaven. If you die without confessing you are a sinner, you will be eternally separated from God. Furthermore, you will miss out on God's best blessings for your life.

God wants to forgive your sins so that you can receive salvation and experience His best for you. The "Roman Road to Salvation" follows:

- "For all have sinned and fall short of the glory of God" (Romans 3:23).

- "For the wages of sin is death, but the free gift of God is eternal life in Christ Jesus our Lord" (Romans 6:23).
- "But God demonstrates His own love toward us, in that while we were yet sinners, Christ died for us" (Romans 5:8).
- "for "WHOEVER WILL CALL ON THE NAME OF THE LORD WILL BE SAVED" (Romans 10:13).
- "If you confess with your mouth Jesus as Lord, and believe in your heart that God raised Him from the dead, you will be saved; for with the heart a person believes, resulting in righteousness, and with the mouth he confesses, resulting in salvation" (Romans 10:9–10).

We are born with a sinful nature and naturally gravitate towards sin. The Bible clearly states that our sins must be paid for: the "wages of sin is death." Although we cannot pay for our own sins, God loves us so much that He sent His son Jesus Christ to die on the cross to pay for our sins. On the third day following the crucifixion, God resurrected Jesus from the dead.

Salvation is God's gift to you based solely on His grace. **To be forgiven and to receive salvation, confess you are a sinner, acknowledge that Jesus died on the cross to pay for your sins, and believe that He arose from the dead on the third day.**

Embrace God's Plan for Your Life

Once you have accepted Jesus Christ as your Lord and Savior, embrace God's plan to experience an abundant and successful life. God tells us through the prophet Jeremiah: "'For I know the plans that I have for you,' declares the Lord, 'plans for welfare and not for calamity to give you a future and a hope'" (Jeremiah 29:11). (Note that "welfare" in this context means blessing!)

Think about that. **The Creator of the universe has a great plan for your life.** The apostle Paul reminds us: "And God is able to make all grace abound to you, so that always having all sufficiency in everything, you may have an abundance for every good deed" (2 Corinthians 9:8). God already has mapped out a plan for your life. The Psalmist tells us that, "The steps of a man are established by the Lord, And He delights in his way. 24When he falls, he will not be hurled headlong, because the Lord is the One who holds his hand" (Psalm 37:23–24). When you follow God's plan for your life, and are obedient to Him, He will guide you and work powerfully in your life.

Of course, before you can embrace God's plan for your life, you must know God's plan for your life. Pray to God and ask Him to reveal His plan. You can be confident that God will communicate with you: "Call to Me and I will answer you, and I will tell you great and mighty things, which you do not know" (Jeremiah 33:3). God promises His children: "He will call on me, and I will answer him" (Psalm 91:15). Prayer is a powerful tool for Christians. Remember what the apostle Paul says and always "Pray without ceasing" (1 Thessalonians 5:17). When you do pray, you can be sure that "The effective prayer of a righteous man can accomplish much" (James 5:16).

Although God generally reveals His plan in small increments, you can be sure that His plan includes abundance. In John 10:10 Jesus states, "I came that they may have life, and have it abundantly." Many Christians believe that God's promise of abundance guarantees abundant money and possessions. This belief is not correct. The apostle Paul assures us that: "And my God will supply all your needs according to His riches in glory in Christ Jesus" (Philippians 4:19). God will provide what you need but does not promise to make you rich. **Christians, though, can have spiritual abundance: joy, peace, grace, strength, wisdom, mercy, blessing, favor, provision, and protection.**

God's abundance is sufficient for every situation you face. Challenges come to Christians as well as to others, but Christians have God's abundant strength, peace, and hope to handle every challenge. The apostle Paul, writing from prison, states, "¹²I know how to get along with humble means, and I also know how to live in prosperity; in any and every circumstance I have learned the secret of being filled and going hungry, both of having abundance and suffering need. ¹³I can do all things through Him who strengthens me" (Philippians 4:12-13).

God knows (even if you don't) that you need His help. **Seek Him, and He will empower you.** God tells us through the prophet Isaiah: "Do not fear, for I am with you; Do not anxiously look about you, for I am your God. I will strengthen you, surely I will help you, surely I will uphold you with My righteous right hand" (Isaiah 41:10). I have memorized this verse, and I encourage you to memorize it as well. Pray when you need God's strength: "Father God, You told me not to fear, not to be anxious. You said You would strengthen me and help me. You said You would uphold me. I need Your strength!"

Obey and be Blessed

You must obey God to experience an abundant and successful life. **Salvation is unconditional, but blessings are not.** God spoke through the prophet Jeremiah to emphasize the importance of obedience: "But this is what I commanded them, saying, 'Obey My voice, and I will be your God, and you will be My people; and you will walk in all the way which I command you, that it may be well with you" (Jeremiah 7:23). **You "walk in all the way in which I command" by doing what God tells you to do,** and you do what God tells you to do by relying on His strength. Additionally, **you "walk in all the way in which I command" by avoiding willful sin,** and you avoid willful sin by believing that: "No temptation has overtaken you but such as is common to man;

and God is faithful, who will not allow you to be tempted beyond what you are able, but with the temptation will provide the way of escape also, so that you will be able to endure it" (1 Corinthians 10:13). **You can overcome temptation if you rely on God's strength rather than your own.** When you feel tempted by sin, ask God to show you how to escape.

The Bible gives a great illustration of blessing following obedience. The apostle Peter, known also as Simon, was a fisherman. Jesus had been speaking to a crowd from Simon's fishing boat:

> ⁴When He had finished speaking, He said to Simon, 'Put out into the deep water and let down your nets for a catch.' ⁵Simon answered and said, 'Master, we worked hard all night and caught nothing, but I will do as You say and let down the nets.' ⁶When they had done this, they enclosed a great quantity of fish, and their nets began to break; ⁷so they signaled to their partners in the other boat for them to come and help them. And they came and filled both of the boats, so that they began to sink (Luke 5:4-7).

These verses illustrate important principles. First, **Simon obeyed Jesus and was blessed** with a "great quantity" of fish. Secondly, Simon obeyed Jesus even though his experience as a fisherman suggested that doing so would be a waste of time. You also may sense God telling you to do something that does not make sense. **You don't need to understand why God tells you to do something; you just need to do it.** (See Proverbs 3:5 below.) I don't recommend that you always follow advice from people when their advice does not make sense to you. But **you can trust completely the sovereign God of the universe to tell you what is best for you, and you will be blessed when you obey.**

Note also that Simon called his fishing buddies to join in. They "filled their boats" too. **Not only will God bless your obedience, but He often will bless others through you.**

In this example, Simon was not looking for a blessing. However, God tells us: "All these blessings will come upon you and overtake you if you obey the Lord your God" (Deuteronomy 28:2). Conversely, "If you do not obey the Lord your God, to observe to do all His commandments and His statutes with which I charge you today, that all these curses will come upon you and overtake you" (Deuteronomy 28:15).

Will blessings really "overtake you?" Returning to my office after a meeting one day, I had a message to call a person I did not know. I called her, and she said that her college was hiring a new leader for its academic programs. She asked me if I was interested in the position and encouraged me to apply. I was interested because of my affinity for her university. However, I was happy with my current job. I sought advice from my mentor and a few colleagues. The consensus was that I should apply for the job but not tell my boss I was applying. I trusted my colleagues and mentor, but I prayed and believed God was telling me to inform my boss that I was considering the other job.

Following God's prompting, I told my boss that I was considering applying for the other job. My boss was supportive but told me to put together a list of things he could do to keep me from applying. I gave the list to my boss, and I got everything I asked for, including a raise that would have taken more than four years of typical annual salary increases to achieve.

If I would have asked my boss for that big raise without the other job prospect, he would have laughed at me. I was not looking for another job, but God set me up for a blessing; in other words, this blessing "overtook" me. And the blessing was in response to obedience. Had I disregarded God's prompting, I would not have told my boss about the other job, and I would not have received the blessing.

Stay Faithful

Stay faithful and believe that God will empower you to experience an abundant and successful life. Jesus tells us in Matthew 17:20, "If you have faith the size of a mustard seed, you will say to this mountain, 'Move from here to there,' and it will move; and nothing will be impossible to you." **Even if you can't see how God can provide for you or help you, have faith.** As stated in Proverbs 3:5: "Trust in the Lord with all your heart and do not lean on your own understanding. In all your ways acknowledge Him, And He will make your paths straight."

Your life's journey likely will be more challenging than you think it should be. It likely will include detours, heartaches, setbacks, and obstacles that you would prefer to avoid. **If you remain faithful, God will work out His plan in your life. But understand that He will do it His way and on His schedule.** When you stay in faith, God will be glorified, and you will be blessed: "20Now to Him who is able to do far more abundantly beyond all that we ask or think, according to the power that works within us, 21to Him be the glory in the church and in Christ Jesus to all generations forever and ever. Amen" (Ephesians 3:20–21).

Let me share a personal example showing the importance of staying in faith while God works His plan. My wife informed me one day that I was going to be a dad. We were very excited, but the excitement gave way to despair as we suffered a miscarriage. We were devastated. Soon, we were expecting a baby again. The joy returned, and then the despair returned as we suffered another miscarriage. We spent thousands of dollars on a series of fertility treatments over the next couple of years. I came to refer to the treatments as "futility treatments" rather than "fertility treatments" because they did not work for us.

At this point, I was about done with God and His plan for my life. After all, I had been praying for a child, and God was not honoring my request. I was complaining about this to a trusted Christian friend, and he told me, "One day you have to decide whether or not you really trust God." His comment hit me hard. I realized that God was God, and I was not. I realized that my faith was weak, and that I should seek God's plan rather than tell Him to honor my plan. I further realized that my prayers had been superficial and selfish.

I asked God to forgive my selfishness. I asked God to give us a child according to His will, if His will was for us to have children. We soon believed that we were supposed to adopt an international child. The adoption process took almost four years, but now we have a beautiful daughter.

Our journey to parenthood took longer than I thought it should have. We experienced numerous setbacks and intense heartache that we would have preferred to avoid. Through it all, God was faithful, and He provided a child—on His schedule and according to His plan. I still don't understand His plan, but I don't need to understand His plan. I do understand that now we have a child, and a wonderful little girl has a loving Mom and Dad. I understand that God is in charge, and I need to honor Him. And I understand that Romans 8:28 is absolutely true: "And we know that God causes all things to work together for good to those who love God, to those who are called according to His purpose."

I struggled in the midst of our suffering to see how God could possibly work things together for good, but He did. When you find yourself in a situation that appears hopeless or when you face a seemingly insurmountable obstacle, remember how God worked in our situation. Believe that He will work in your situation as well. Stay faithful!

Now that you see how Christians are divinely empowered to succeed, you are ready to develop the leadership and soft skills needed for your success. The next section provides an overview of these skills.

An Overview of the 3Rs

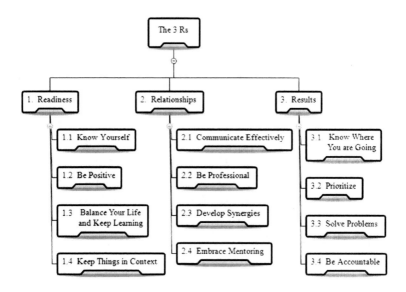

As stated in the Introduction, I teach leadership and soft skills by using the 3Rs, *Readiness, Relationships,* and *Results.* The 3Rs represent focus areas on which to develop your leadership and soft skills. Each area includes several key abilities, behaviors, and attitudes.

Readiness

The first R stands for *Readiness* and includes the following:

1. Knowing yourself
2. Being positive
3. Committing to life balance and lifelong learning
4. Keeping things in the proper context

In this book, I discuss *Readiness* in terms of being prepared to handle whatever comes your way. You must be ready to take advantage of opportunities and handle occasional setbacks if you want to be successful. My expectation is that you will be ready, and that you will continue to grow and ultimately achieve the abundant and successful life that God has planned for you. To be ready, you must know yourself, be positive, commit to life balance and lifelong learning, and keep things in the proper context.

Knowing yourself means that you are self-aware and know your strengths and weaknesses. God has given you strengths, and you are more effective when working in your areas of strength. Similarly, you must recognize and manage your weaknesses. When you evaluate your weaknesses, you may find that many weaknesses can be overcome by working harder and smarter. Understand that **God can demonstrate His strength through your weaknesses.**

Knowing yourself also means you understand that **God is the ultimate source of your strength.** God will use challenging experiences to teach you to rely on Him. When you pray for His help, God will sharpen your skills and you will gain greater confidence in Him. As your skill level and confidence in God grow, you will be ready for greater opportunities. Be sure to prayerfully reflect on your challenging experiences. Indeed, **experience is a great teacher, but only if you reflect and learn from your experiences.**

Attitude is a critically important component of *Readiness*. Your attitude has a great influence on your relationships, productivity, and happiness. If you want to be a successful leader, learn to maintain a positive attitude; this attitude will inspire and encourage the people around you. Furthermore, the right attitude will help you overcome setbacks and struggles. The wrong attitude can damage your relationships and undermine your skills. To maintain a positive attitude, trust in God, focus on your opportunities, and surround yourself with positive people.

Readiness requires a commitment to life balance and lifelong learning. If your life is out of balance, long-term success and happiness will be difficult to achieve. Balance is achieved when you spend quality time in each of the important areas of your life. Furthermore, if you want continued success, you must look for and take advantage of opportunities to learn throughout your life.

Readiness requires that you keep things in context so you don't lose sight of your overall goals. If you lose sight, you can burn out and want to give up. Keep focused on your big goals while working on the small (and occasionally boring) steps along the way to your goal. Maintaining the proper context can also help you stay motivated after a loss or setback. As a Christian, your overall context is your identity as a child of God. Don't let a failure or setback cause you to lose your focus. Avoid focusing on what knocked you down; focus on what you can achieve. Be a cannon ball and blast through life's obstacles.

Readiness focuses on you. In Part II, we discuss *Relationships*, which focuses on your ability to build productive connections and work effectively with family, friends, and team members. By applying what you learned in *Readiness,* you will be more effective in your *Relationships.*

Relationships

The second R stands for *Relationships* and includes the following:

1. Effective communication
2. Professionalism
3. Synergy
4. Mentoring

Relationships are very important in your personal and professional life. Your personal relationship with Jesus Christ is your most important relationship. The quality of your relationships often determines the quality of your life. Similarly, your professional relationships and network of colleagues often determines your success at work. Successful people excel on the job and they also build strong relationships. Our discussion of relationships includes effective communication, professionalism, synergy, and mentoring.

Effective communication skills are essential for strong relationships. An effective communicator focuses on the person he is communicating with rather than on himself. Doing so requires clarity and an understanding of what is important to others. Furthermore, effective communicators are good listeners. They also encourage others and show appreciation. Effective leaders must be effective communicators.

Professionalism is another key aspect of building effective relationships. A professional is a person who is competent and is a good communicator. Professionals see beyond differences and work effectively with diverse groups of people. Professionals are strongly committed to high integrity and always honor their commitments. When your integrity is high and you follow through, people around you will quickly learn that they can trust you. Trust is foundational to effective relationships. Christians are more effective ambassadors for Jesus Christ when they display professionalism.

Synergy is an outcome of effective relationships and refers to the ability of people working together to achieve more than do people working alone. Synergy is greater on teams that are diverse in expertise, perspective, and experience. Christians experience maximum synergy by trusting God to work in and through their lives.

When working with others, always know who is responsible for doing what and by when it is supposed to be done. Furthermore, each person must work on his or her responsibilities. And remember that you should not expect your boss to solve all of your problems. If you do take a problem to your boss for help, take a few solutions as well.

We end our discussion on *Relationships* with mentoring. You greatly improve your likelihood for success by finding a mentor who can help you make wise decisions, develop needed skills, and work through obstacles. Jesus is the ultimate mentor for Christians. To benefit from mentoring, be willing to listen and apply what you learn. Furthermore, you can help others grow as you share your experiences with them.

Readiness focuses on you as an individual. *Relationships* focuses on your connections with others. Part III focuses on *Results*, getting the job done. The ability to get the job done is absolutely essential to your success, regardless of what the job is.

Results

The third R stands for *Results*, and includes the following:

1. Knowledge of where you are going
2. Ability to prioritize
3. Ability to solve problems
4. Willingness to be accountable

If you want to be successful, be future-oriented and focus on *Results*. Producing results is not the same as being busy. You must understand the difference between doing something and doing something important. Many people are busy all the time but produce nothing of value. To produce something valuable, you must know where you are going, focus on your priorities, solve problems, and be accountable.

Knowing where you are going means that you know what is important to you, as defined by God's plan for your life. If you don't know God's plan for your life, you will waste time chasing insignificant things. You might be busy, but you won't achieve meaningful goals. Setting and achieving meaningful goals requires you to anchor your goals to your God-given values. If your goals are not anchored to your values, you won't work hard enough to achieve the goal. Or if you do achieve the goal, it won't really matter because it is not part of God's plan for you.

Once you set goals based on what is important to you (based on God's plan for your life), prioritize your time and focus your effort to achieve those goals. Strive to invest your time on your priorities rather than merely being busy. Understand that everything is not important. Spending time on things that are not important will prevent you from spending time on your priorities. Protect your time from urgent but unimportant activities, and don't let someone else's priorities knock you off-course.

Problem solving should be a priority for you. Whether in your family, school, or work, you must solve problems if you are going to be successful. You must develop the ability to clearly define a problem. It has been said that once you have defined a problem, you have it half-solved. God promises to give you wisdom, and you can use His wisdom to define and solve problems. Furthermore, solving problems will increase your influence. The greater your influence, the greater your potential for opportunity, rewards, and success.

The final section of *Results*, and of the entire book, is accountability. To be successful, take responsibility for your attitude, effort, behavior, work, and even for your mistakes. Christians are accountable to God and to fellow Christians. Be accountable to yourself as well, always putting forth your best effort, and always doing your very best work. I have seen many young people fail to achieve what they could achieve due to their lack of effort. Christians can call on God to empower them to do their best work. Finally, accountability requires you to admit your mistakes, learn from them, and then move on.

Part I: Readiness

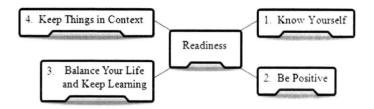

In the Gospel of Matthew, we read about the importance of being ready: "⁴²Therefore be on the alert, for you do not know which day your Lord is coming. ⁴³But be sure of this, that if the head of the house had known at what time of the night the thief was coming, he would have been on the alert and would not have allowed his house to be broken into. ⁴⁴For this reason you also must be ready; for the Son of Man is coming at an hour when you do not think He will" (Matthew 24:42-44).

The context of this passage is that Christians should be ready for the Second Coming of Jesus Christ. The principle of readiness applies to other aspects of your life as well. Indeed, you will be more successful if you are ready to take advantage of the opportunities that God provides to you. Similarly, you must be ready to handle difficulties that come your way.

Although being ready makes sense, I have seen many young people "wing it." In other words, rather than working hard to prepare, they just put forth minimal effort and hope for the best. At worst, some put forth no effort and don't worry about the results. For example, rather than studying adequately for a test, a student goes in unprepared and wings it. Rather than working hard on a project on the job, an employee just wings it. If you wing it and are not ready, you may not fail, but you likely won't do your best work. As will be discussed later, always pray that God empowers you to do your best work, and never let your performance be limited by a lack of effort.

You may think that you have been pretty successful winging it so far in your life. And perhaps you have. However, I assure you that as you progress through life, winging it will not always work. Readiness and preparation will be more important as you advance in your education and career. You should plan to work harder in college than you did in high school, and you likely will work harder in your job than you did in college.

The bottom line is that you must be ready to take advantage of opportunities, to overcome challenges, and to do what it takes to reach your goals. Rely on God's strength rather than your own and develop your leadership and soft skills; doing so will enhance your readiness.

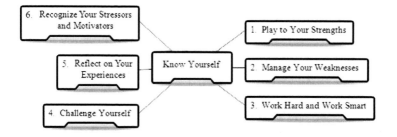

6. Recognize Your Stressors and Motivators

1. Play to Your Strengths

5. Reflect on Your Experiences

Know Yourself

2. Manage Your Weaknesses

4. Challenge Yourself

3. Work Hard and Work Smart

Chapter 1: Know Yourself

To take advantage of your opportunities and overcome difficulties, you must truly know yourself. God has given each of us skills, abilities, and perspectives that allow us to make unique contributions. **The better you recognize your strengths and your unique ability to make a difference, the more ready you will be to leverage your opportunities.** But your strengths will help you only if you use them! The apostle Peter says: "[10]As each one has received a special gift, employ it in serving one another as good stewards of the manifold grace of God. [11]Whoever speaks, is to do so as one who is speaking the utterances of God; whoever serves is to do so as one who is serving by the strength which God supplies; so that in all things God may be glorified through Jesus Christ, to whom belongs the glory and dominion forever and ever" (1 Peter 4:10-11). Note that these verses say, "Employ it" and "Do so"—you are called to use the strengths that God gave you.

A colleague of mine has a program he calls "The I in Team." You probably have heard that there is no "I" in team. However, my colleague teaches that each individual team member must contribute to the overall success of the team; use your unique strengths to contribute to your team. Don't misinterpret this "I" in team as being the star, but use your strengths so that your team succeeds. By making strong contributions to a successful team, you set yourself up for opportunities as an individual.

Play to Your Strengths

How do you identify your strengths? A full assessment of your strengths and weaknesses is beyond the scope of this book, but the following questions will give you insight:

1. What do you think your strengths are?

2. What do your friends tell you that your strengths are? (Ask three or four friends.)

3. What do you enjoy doing?

4. What do people ask you to do?

You likely have strengths that are not developed fully, and you likely have strengths that have not been identified by the questions above. Ask God to reveal your strengths to you. I encourage you to find a book or assessment that can help you determine your strengths. There are several good resources available online; one of the best is Strengthfinders.com. If you are a student, contact your advisor or counselor to identify resources. Ask your mentor what he sees as your strengths. Don't forget that as a Christian, God's power in your life is a divine strength!

Please list your strengths below:

1.

2.

3.

4.

5.

By definition, your strengths help you succeed if you utilize them. Describe below ways to leverage your strengths to enhance your leadership and soft skills. For example, if you have a great attitude and encourage others, people naturally will gravitate towards you. Your positive influence on others will increase your leadership potential.

Please provide examples of how you can use your strengths.

1.

2.

3.

4.

5.

Manage Your Weaknesses

As a Christian, you know you were created by God. Why, then, would you have weaknesses? The apostle Paul says: "And He has said to me, 'My grace is sufficient for you, for power is perfected in weakness.' Most gladly, therefore, I will rather boast about my weaknesses, so that the power of Christ may dwell in me" (2 Corinthians 12:9).

God demonstrates His power in your weaknesses. As you experience God's power in your life, you gain greater confidence in Him. As your confidence in God grows, He will use you for greater and greater works.

To begin identifying your weaknesses, answer the following questions:

1. What do you think your weaknesses are?

2. What do your friends tell you your weaknesses are? (Ask three or four friends.)

3. What do you try to avoid doing? (We often avoid areas of weakness.)

4. What has caused you to fail to complete a task or to do less than your best work?

5. What has caused problems in your relationships?

My areas for improvement are:

1.

2.

3.

4.

5.

Now that you have identified a few areas for improvement, how do you manage these areas? The obvious answer is to improve. Generally, improvement is the best approach. For example, if you often fail to complete assignments, often get your work done late, or if you frequently rush through your tasks and fail to produce quality work, you likely have a weakness in time management. If you do not improve your ability to manage your time, you diminish your ability to succeed.

Following are some steps you can take to improve your weaknesses:

1. Identify your weakness.

2. Believe you can improve.

3. Find resources.

4. Make a plan to improve.

5. Define the impact.

6. Put forth real effort.

7. Assess your progress.

8. Celebrate your progress.

The first step, of course, is to identify your weakness. Then truly believe you can improve the weakness. Next, find resources, tools, and techniques that others used to overcome the same weakness. These resources may include books and websites, or perhaps a seminar. If you have a mentor, ask her for advice. Ask God for His guidance.

Using the information from the resources, make a plan for improvement. Be sure to define the impact: How will improving the weakness benefit you? Be clear when describing the impact. Refer to your impact statement regularly to stay motivated. Finally, work through your plan and periodically assess your progress. Realize that even small improvements represent progress. Celebrate your progress, and don't be discouraged if the process takes longer than you think it should.

Using the steps outlined above, let me share an example of how I am overcoming my weakness of perfectionism: I identified my weakness when I found myself with several projects that were almost finished. I knew I could finish the projects if I could get over my need for perfection. I sought out the advice of a mentor, and she gave me some practical tools to use. She started out with an example of brushing my teeth. She asked if I brushed my teeth all day. I told her that I did not. She said, "Of course you don't. You decide when you have done your best, and then you move on." She encouraged me to use the same approach on my projects. For each project, I must decide when I have done enough work to satisfy the goal of the project, rather than putting in additional time that ultimately does little to improve the project. I took her advice and finished several projects, which freed up time for other things. My outcomes were that I was getting more work done, and I was maintaining the quality of my work. I still must deliberately guard against perfectionism, but I am making great progress. You, too, can make progress if you follow the steps listed above.

As a Christian, ask God to equip you in the midst of your weakness. When God instructed Moses and his brother Aaron to tell the Pharaoh to set the Israelites free, Moses was worried about his inability to communicate. God told Moses that He would equip them and tell them what to say. In Exodus 4:15 God said, "You are to speak to him and put the words in his mouth; and I, even I, will be with your mouth and his mouth, and I will teach you what you are to do."

You also can manage your weaknesses by letting someone else cover for you. To overcome Moses' perceived inability to speak, God used Aaron to speak for Moses: "Moreover, he shall speak for you to the people; and he will be as a mouth for you and you will be as God to him" (Exodus 4:16).

Similarly, if you have strength in planning an event, but are a weak public speaker, let someone on your team present your plan. You also may ask your teammate to mentor you as she prepares and delivers the presentation. Someday, you may be able to hire people who complement your strengths and weaknesses and then delegate these tasks to them.

What if your weakness is not limiting you? In this case, don't worry about it. Perhaps you are not a good athlete or are not especially artistic. One of my weaknesses, among many, is that I can't sing. I was asked to fill in for a singer in our church's praise band for a couple weeks. That was several years ago, and I have not been asked to do it again. If I chose to, I could dwell on the fact that I can't sing. However, that weakness is not keeping me from reaching my goals, so I choose not to worry about it.

Here is my point: If you have a weakness in an area that is not required for your relationships, school work, or employment, the weakness may not be worth addressing. I have known some people who keep a mental list of things they can't do and then dwell on the fact that they can't do them. Don't stress yourself worrying about a weakness that is not limiting you. A word of caution, however: Before dismissing a weakness, seek God's guidance through prayer and be sure that the weakness is not diminishing your effectiveness or limiting your ability to move ahead.

Realize that some weaknesses may be over-expressed strengths. Think back to my example of overcoming perfectionism. A strength of mine is the desire to do my best work. However, I often over-express that strength as perfectionism. Sometimes, I won't finish a project until I think it is perfect. Taken to the extreme, the project never gets done. Failing to complete projects for this reason is a weakness, but the weakness is rooted in a strength. My competitiveness also can be over-expressed to the point that sometimes I focus solely on results rather than on people, and this tendency can be a real weakness in relationships. Reflecting on your weaknesses can help you identify when you are doing too much of a good thing to the point that your effectiveness is diminished.

I want you to consider a few other points in our discussion of weaknesses. I have heard many students say, "I am no good in math," "I can't ever get to class on time," "I can never get my homework done on time," or "I will never understand chemistry"….the list goes on and on. I challenge you, if you have ever taken this approach, not to give in so easily. Indeed, these statements likely are nothing more than excuses for not trying. Don't settle for that. If you don't understand chemistry (and it certainly did not come easily for me), find a tutor. Pray for understanding. Put more time into it; work lots of homework problems. **Do not consider something to be a weakness until you have put forth your very best effort.** We will discuss this further in the next section.

Work Hard and Work Smart

An apparent weakness in ability may be overcome with deliberate effort and/or by learning new skills. I have seen many young people who feel they have a weakness holding them back discover that the weakness actually represents the need to work harder or smarter.

As a Christian, God will empower you to do what He calls you to do. But relying on God does not exempt you from working hard. King Solomon tells us: "Whatever your hand finds to do, do it with all your might; for there is no activity or planning or knowledge or wisdom in Sheol where you are going" (Ecclesiastes 9:10). He also tells us: "In all labor there is profit, But mere talk leads only to poverty" (Proverbs 14:23).

I had to call on God's strength to succeed in college. My first year in college was nearly my last year in college. I had sailed through high school with success and naturally assumed I would succeed in college. However, I got a "D" in chemistry my first semester. This was difficult for me given my experience in high school, and I nearly dropped out of college. I assumed that a weakness of mine was the inability to succeed in college. Fortunately, I decided to try again. I began to pray more intensely to God for help, took the course over, and got an "A." I took the second chemistry course and got an "A." I went on to get an "A" in physical chemistry in graduate school. This course was arguably the hardest course I ever took, but I got an "A." The point is I had to change my study habits and work ethic, and I had to learn how to manage my time. I had the potential, but I had to work harder and smarter to realize it. My weakness was not my perceived lack of ability. Basically, I had to grow up and learn to apply myself to my coursework. I also needed to improve my note-taking and study skills. Given that I was able to succeed by retaking the course and also by doing well in subsequent courses, I learned a valuable lesson: College was not easy, but I could handle it if I tapped into God's strength and worked harder and smarter.

Don't underestimate the need to work smarter as well as harder. You must learn new skills to conquer new challenges. In the chemistry class example, I needed to develop better skills in note-taking, studying, and time management. Working hard is crucial but is often not enough. If you don't realize this fact, you may work harder but not get the results you want, which can lead to frustration and cause you to give up.

God will help you if you humble yourself and ask Him. You undoubtedly will encounter new challenges as you progress into new phases of your life. **Once you know yourself and understand your abilities, and as you call on God to strengthen you, you will be ready to conquer increasingly difficult challenges.** I have heard it said that difficult challenges don't bother us nearly as much as do *unexpected* difficult challenges. The apostle Peter tells us that we should not be surprised by difficult challenges in life: "Beloved, do not be surprised at the fiery ordeal among you, which comes upon you for your testing, as though some strange thing were happening to you" (1 Peter 4:12).

Early Christians faced "fiery ordeals" due to their faith in Jesus Christ. However, God can and will use various trials in many aspects of our lives to teach us and to conform us to His plan. When you face challenges, allow God's power to strengthen you to work harder and smarter until you overcome them.

What if you are working harder and smarter but still struggle? Ask God what He wants to tell you. Struggling results in frustration and disappointment, but God can use your struggles to work in your life. As an example, in my career I have taught and mentored many students who wanted to go to veterinary school. However, the admission requirements for veterinary schools are quite high. Thus, the stark reality is that some students who intensely want to get into a veterinary school lack the grades to get admitted.

This reality requires students to change *their* plans and seek another career. Initially, many students see this as a failure. However, in reality, this is not a failure. I have seen several of these students go on to have successful careers in other fields. (Remember Romans 8:28.) **We each have strengths and abilities in some areas, but not in all areas. If you feel confused by your struggles, seek God, and He will tell you what to do.** You can pray: "Father God, You said that You have a plan for my life. Please reveal Your will to me and guide me in the direction You want me to go." You may learn that your struggle is designed to help you grow where you are (recall my chemistry class example). Conversely, He may lead you to change direction, as in the case of some students who lack the grades to get into veterinary school. To help you evaluate what to do, you can also talk to your pastor, mentor, or your school counselor.

Challenge Yourself

Another component of knowing yourself is the willingness to **put yourself in situations that stretch you.** In other words, **challenge yourself.** To truly know yourself, and to see God work in your life, you have to attempt tasks that are challenging or that represent new experiences. The old adage, "You never know until you try," is true. Challenging situations allow God to demonstrate His power in your life. **If everything you attempt to do is easy, you're not challenging yourself, and you are not growing like you otherwise could.**

The importance of stretching is seen in the story of Gideon in the book of Judges. The entire story of Gideon is beyond the scope of this book, and I encourage you to read about Gideon in the book of Judges. Briefly, the Israelites who had been released from Egyptian bondage were suffering terribly due to the Midianites. Israel needed a leader to step up and fight against the Midianites. God sent an angel to tell Gideon to lead the fight: "¹⁴The Lord looked at him and said, 'Go in this your strength and deliver Israel from the hand of Midian. Have I not sent you?' ¹⁵He said to Him, 'O Lord, how shall I deliver Israel? Behold, my family is the least in Manasseh, and I am the youngest in my father's house.' ¹⁶But the Lord said to him, 'Surely I will be with you, and you shall defeat Midian as one man'" (Judges 6:14-16).

Clearly, Gideon did not want to be stretched. He gave several excuses as to why he could not succeed. The angel responded that God would be with Gideon and that Gideon would succeed because God was with him. Gideon did indeed succeed with a stunning victory over the Midianites. Gideon's victory came from God.

Gideon's victory illustrates a Biblical principle that can change your life. **If God calls you to do something, He will equip you to do it. Christians do not succeed because of their own strength. We succeed by letting God work in and through us and by using His inexhaustible power and wisdom.**

Perhaps you have heard the phrase "willing and able." If Christians are willing, God will make them able. A friend of mine often says, "God does not call people who are equipped to do His work. He equips the people He calls to do His work." The writer of Hebrews assures us that God will, "equip you in every good thing to do His will, working in us that which is pleasing in His sight, through Jesus Christ, to whom be the glory forever and ever. Amen" (Hebrews 13:21). Furthermore, the apostle Paul tells us that God provided Scripture, "so that the man of God may be adequate, equipped for every good work" (2 Timothy 3:17). Thus, if you seek God's strength and read God's word, God will equip you to do what He calls you to do.

The Bible contains numerous examples of God empowering people to succeed. As you read the following verses, please understand that God can empower your success as well. It took me awhile to realize this fact. I thought that people in the Bible were special and that God helped them more than He would help me. Actually, many people in the Bible are special; not because they are in the Bible, but because they have placed their faith in God. When you place your faith in God, He will work powerfully in your life just as He did for the people in the Bible.

- "The Lord was with Joseph, so he became a successful man. And he was in the house of his master, the Egyptian" (Genesis 39:2).
- "The chief jailer did not supervise anything under Joseph's charge because the Lord was with him; and whatever he did, the Lord made to prosper" (Genesis 39:23).
- "David was prospering in all his ways for the Lord was with him" (1 Samuel 18:14).
- "So the Lord was with Joshua, and his fame was in all the land" (Joshua 6:27).
- "And the Lord was with him; wherever he went he prospered. And he rebelled against the king of Assyria and did not serve him" (2 Kings 18:7).

Let's take this a step further. When you place your faith in Jesus Christ, He sends the Holy Spirit (Spirit of Truth, Helper) to live in your heart. The Holy Spirit will guide you, strengthen you, and enable you to do extraordinary things. The following verses describe the Holy Spirit in the lives of Christians:

- "In Him, you also, after listening to the message of truth, the gospel of your salvation— having also believed, you were sealed in Him with the Holy Spirit of promise" (Ephesians 1:13).
- "Truly, truly, I say to you, he who believes in Me, the works that I do, he will do also; and greater works than these he will do; because I go to the Father" (John 14:12).
- "I will ask the Father, and He will give you another Helper, that He may be with you forever" (John 14:16).
- "But the Helper, the Holy Spirit, whom the Father will send in My name, He will teach you all things, and bring to your remembrance all that I said to you" (John 14:26).
- "But I tell you the truth, it is to your advantage that I go away; for if I do not go away, the Helper will not come to you; but if I go, I will send Him to you" (John 16:7).
- "But when He, the Spirit of truth, comes, He will guide you into all the truth; for He will not speak on His own initiative, but whatever He hears, He will speak; and He will disclose to you what is to come" (John 16:13).

You receive the Holy Spirit when you receive your salvation. So, if you have confessed that you are a sinner and have accepted Jesus Christ as your Lord and Savior, the Holy Spirit lives in you. Jesus emphasized that it is "to your advantage" that He is going to His Father so that the Holy Spirit can come to Christians. Jesus also said that the Holy Spirit will guide and enable Christians to do even more than He did. When you call on the Holy Spirit, He will do these things for you.

God will empower you as you tackle activities that stretch you. As long as you have prayed and are sure that God wants you to step up, you can be sure that God will equip you to do what He calls you to do. As Joshua began to lead the Israelites after the death of Moses, God told Joshua three times to be strong and courageous:

- "Be strong and courageous, for you shall give this people possession of the land which I swore to their fathers to give them" (Joshua 1:6).
- "Only be strong and very courageous; be careful to do according to all the law which Moses My servant commanded you; do not turn from it to the right or to the left, so that you may have success wherever you go." (Joshua 1:7).
- "Have I not commanded you? Be strong and courageous! Do not tremble or be dismayed, for the LORD your God is with you wherever you go" (Joshua 1:9).

If God says something three times, you need to pay attention, believe it, and act on it. God is telling you to be "strong and courageous" as you walk according to His guidance. Maybe you "tremble" sometimes and don't think you are a strong and courageous person. If so, remember that strength and courage come not from you, but from God who promises to be with you as you follow His plan.

Let me illustrate how a stretching opportunity helped me. When I was a senior in college, I took a graduate-level course. There were fifteen students in the class, and I was the only undergraduate. Because all the other students were more advanced than I and were pursuing masters and doctoral degrees, I was intimidated. In fact, I thought I would get the lowest grade in the class. (I was not a great man of faith at that time.) However, a graduate student and I soon became friends, and he asked for my help. He was an older-than-average student who had not had chemistry in ten years, and I tutored him on chemistry. Furthermore, I earned an "A" in this class. More importantly, I learned I could succeed in graduate-level courses. Succeeding in this challenging course gave me the confidence to take on other challenges. Thus, even though I had the wrong expectation about my grade and was intimidated by the level of the class, I stepped up to a challenge that stretched me, gave me good experience, and taught me a valuable lesson. Even though my faith was not particularly strong, God's strength gave me success in the class.

Ask God to reveal three potential activities or opportunities that could stretch you:

1.

2.

3.

Make a commitment to follow through on each of these activities. Share this list with a friend or a mentor to keep you accountable. As you engage in these stretching activities, realize that you may not succeed on your first attempt, and that's OK. Be sure to call on God for help, and realize that He may teach you something through an occasional setback. If you do experience a setback, ask God what He wants you to learn. Make any changes He tells you to make, and remain committed to keep trying until you succeed. When you do succeed, you gain skills, experience, and confidence in God that will allow you to tackle future challenges.

After you complete your stretching activities, reflect on the experience and answer the following questions:

1. What were you most worried about with this activity?

2. How did you expect that activity to cause you to grow as a leader?

3. What was the most difficult aspect of this activity?

4. What did you learn about yourself as you stepped up to this activity?

5. Describe how this activity helped you grow.

I challenge you to live your life such that you achieve everything that God has planned for you. To do this, you must stretch yourself; when you do, you may have some setbacks. But they will be temporary, and you will learn from them. Keep in mind that even if you don't achieve your goal, you will learn something and gain experience that will help you in the future. A mistake is only a mistake if nothing is learned from it. Thus, strive to learn something from each of your setbacks by prayerfully reflecting on the experience. Finally, remember God's promise in Romans 8:28: "And we know that God causes all things to work together for good to those who love God, to those who are called according to His purpose." Please note that this promise requires that you love God and follow His purpose!

Reflect on Your Experiences

Reflection is a key process in knowing yourself. Reflection is the process of thinking deeply in retrospect to gain insight. When you finish something, prayerfully think back over what you did and determine what you could have done differently, how you could do it better next time, and what you learned that you can use in the future. You also may reflect on your values from time to time to focus on what is really important to you. You certainly must reflect on God's plan for your life to be sure you are working toward His goals.

We read in Psalm 119:59: "I considered my ways and turned my feet to your testimonies." The Psalmist reflected on his experiences and determined that he needed to make a change. If you don't reflect on your experiences, you may continue down the wrong path or may continue to make the same mistakes. The apostle Paul states: "Pay close attention to yourself and to your teaching; persevere in these things, for as you do this you will ensure salvation both for yourself and for those who hear you" (1 Timothy 4:16). Note that Paul says you are to pay attention to yourself and your work (teaching in this case).

Reflect on your successes and on your experiences that are not successful. Although it has been said that experience is the best teacher, it also has been said that experience is the best teacher only if you learn from your experience. **To learn from your experiences, be deliberate about reflection and use the insight you gained for future endeavors.** With a little practice, reflection will become second-nature. Ask God to reveal what you need to know.

I constantly emphasize the need for reflection to the young people I work with. I tell them that every project they work on has two very important outcomes. The first outcome is the successful completion of the project itself. The second outcome, which is just as important, is the knowledge gained while working on the project. For example, assume you are planning a volunteer event: The first outcome is the volunteer event itself and the work done by the volunteers. The second outcome is the knowledge and experience gained that will help you plan future events. Perhaps as you planned the volunteer event, you learned that you ran out of time and that you should start earlier when you plan other events. The knowledge and experience gained are real outcomes because you can use them in the future. However, if you are not deliberately reflective, you may not learn fully from the experience. To deliberately reflect, consider these questions:

1.　What worked well?

2. What did not work?

3. What would I do differently if I repeated the project?

4. What did I learn that I can apply to my next project?

I encourage you to write your answers in a journal. As your journaling continues, you can identify your beneficial and detrimental patterns. Addressing detrimental patterns can make a real difference in your ability to grow as a leader. For example, you may see the pattern of frequently missed deadlines; potential solutions to this problem include starting earlier, developing and sticking to a timeline, and staying focused. **If you are not deliberately reflective, you may not see the patterns, and you may continue to make the same mistakes.**

Furthermore, you can pass along your reflection journal to others. For example, if you are an officer in an organization at your school, you can pass your journal to the person who will have your position next year. The information in your journal will help the new officer succeed and will help your organization improve every year.

Recognize Your Stressors and Motivators

The ability to recognize your indicators of stress, fatigue, and overwork is another important component of knowing yourself. Too often, I have wasted time and frustrated myself and others by pushing on when I needed to take a break. My signs of stress are fatigue, impatience, and a condescending tone. When I find myself exhibiting these symptoms, I know it is time to back off, get some exercise, get some rest, and rejuvenate myself. Then, when I get back to the task, I am more efficient.

I can illustrate this with the example of preparing for my preliminary examinations in graduate school. These examinations are a cornerstone of the PhD program. In short, a PhD student gets questioned by five professors for three hours or so. At best, this can be a humbling experience; at worst, you can flunk out of graduate school if you fail the exams. As I prepared for these exams, I spent day and night studying notes, reading books, and scouring scientific manuscripts. Soon, I burned out, was very fatigued, and was not learning much. I studied, but I did not make progress. When I found myself in this situation, I would take a break for a few hours, or even for a day or so. I was much more efficient when I resumed studying. I missed some study time by taking a break, but by rejuvenating myself, I was ready to learn when I returned to studying and ended up making better use of my study time.

Be driven by results, not merely time on task. Make no mistake about it, to achieve your goals, you must expend significant time and effort; however, there are times when you should take a break to rejuvenate yourself.

We read in Genesis 2:2, "By the seventh day God completed His work which He had done, and He rested on the seventh day from all His work which He had done." Why did God rest? Was the Creator of the universe tired? Hardly. He rested because He was done. He also showed the importance of rest to us. The writer of Hebrews tell us, "[9]So there remains a Sabbath rest for the people of God. [10]For the one who has entered His rest has himself also rested from his works, as God did from His" (Hebrews 4:9-10). Furthermore, Jesus tells us, "Come to Me, all who are weary and heavy-laden, and I will give you rest" (Matthew 11:28). God says, "For I satisfy the weary ones and refresh everyone who languishes" (Jeremiah 31:25). **God clearly wants us to experience rest so that we can be rejuvenated.**

It took me awhile to figure this out. In the preliminary examination example above, I felt like I should be studying and could not afford to take a break, even though I was fatigued and was not learning much. I was more focused on the activity of studying (putting time in) than on the outcome of studying (learning). Consider this perspective: If you are a little stressed as you work on something and that stress is motivating you to achieve your goal, you likely can keep working. If, however, the stress is making you unduly worried, causing you to lose sleep and lose focus, or if you are not really accomplishing anything, you should take a break.

Knowing yourself also requires that you understand your motives. Positive motives such as wanting to help someone, improve something, or solve problems should drive you. Negative motives such as pride, greed, anger, or revenge should be avoided. **The motivation behind your actions can be quite insightful and often can help you see when you are investing your time and energy for the wrong reasons.** Our motives are important to God: "All the ways of a man are clean in his own sight, But the Lord weighs the motives" (Proverbs 16:2).

Do you ever find yourself making comments to make yourself look good at the expense of others, or to make others look bad? I remember a quote that my high school baseball coach shared with us: "Class does not build itself up by tearing others down." I have tried to live my life according to this simple statement. However, sometimes I make comments for the wrong reasons with the wrong motives. Doing so damages relationships and can damage your reputation. The fix is quite simple: Know yourself well enough to recognize when your motives are wrong. Pray that God reveals your motives that do not honor Him.

Let me share a situation in which my motive changed from good to bad. I once was in charge of a national competition for students. One of the competitors submitted her project online and assumed the submission was successful. However, unbeknownst to her, the file she submitted became corrupted in the upload process. The judge disqualified the student because he could not open her file. When I learned what had happened (after the deadline for submission), I contacted the judge and asked him to allow the student to resubmit her project. My motives were pure and admirable: I was advocating for a student who was disadvantaged by a situation beyond her control. However, as I talked to the judge, it became clear that he was not going to allow the student to resubmit. We talked quite a bit, and I became angry. Finally, it occurred to me that the discussion was no longer about the student but was now about the fact that the judge was not doing what I wanted him to do.

Clearly, my motives were no longer pure. It hurt my pride (a poor motivator for a Christian), but I finally dropped it. My motive was to "win"— not for the sake of the student, but for my own pride. When I realized that my motivation had changed, I disengaged. The moral of the story: Keep in touch with your motivation for your actions. **Life is too short to waste your time and energy, not to mention your sanity, being driven by unsuitable motives**. And, Christians never should be motivated by pride.

Key points from Chapter 1:

1. God gives you strength to accomplish whatever He calls you to do.

2. Know your strengths and use them to do what God calls you to do.

3. Know your weaknesses and allow God to demonstrate His strength through them.

4. Realize that some weaknesses can be overcome by working harder and smarter.

5. Recognize that you have strengths and abilities in some areas, but not in all areas.

6. Recognize when a "weakness" is just an excuse for not trying.

7. Realize that a weakness may be an over-expressed strength.

8. Embrace situations in which God will stretch you and call on God to strengthen you.

9. Experience is the best teacher only if you learn from it; be reflective.

10. Recognize when you're stressed and need to take a break.

11. God will refresh you when you are weary.

12. Understand your motives.

Please reflect on what you learned in this chapter and answer the following questions:

1. In your own words, explain what it means to know yourself.

2. Why is it important to know yourself?

3. What are the three most significant things you learned from this chapter?

4. List three specific things you will work on to improve your ability to know yourself.

5. What benefit will you experience by following through on the items listed in Question 4?

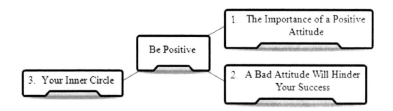

1. The Importance of a Positive Attitude

Be Positive

3. Your Inner Circle

2. A Bad Attitude Will Hinder Your Success

Chapter 2: Be Positive

Christians should be the most positive and joyful people in the world. The reasons we can be positive and joyful are found in Romans 5:1-2: "¹Therefore, having been justified by faith, we have peace with God through our Lord Jesus Christ, ²through whom also we have obtained our introduction by faith into this grace in which we stand; and we exult in hope of the glory of God." **Christians have peace with God, grace, and hope of the glory of God.** If you need another reason to be positive, realize that Jesus said: "Peace I leave with you; My peace I give to you; not as the world gives do I give to you. Do not let your heart be troubled, nor let it be fearful" (John 14:27). **The peace you have through your faith in Jesus Christ is a great source of joy and should give you a very positive attitude.**

Do you realize that no one can take away your joy? **God can give you grace to control your attitude even when you can't control your circumstances.** Although this is a very true statement, it's an easy one to forget. Perhaps you have said, "He makes me mad." However, the hard truth is that no one can make you mad unless you allow the person (or circumstance) to do so.

One summer while in college, I worked as a flagger on a road construction crew. Motorists constantly yelled at me for stopping them. At first, I became angry. Finally, I simply ignored them and stopped getting angry. Through all that, I learned two very powerful lessons: First, there are enough jerks in this world, so I don't need to be one. Second, I could not stop them from yelling at me, but I could stop myself from getting mad.

The Importance of a Positive Attitude

Take a minute and think of a person you admire and with whom you like to spend time. List his or her characteristics below. Then do the same for the person with whom you least like to spend time.

List the characteristics of the person with whom you most want to spend time:

1.

2.

3.

4.

5.

List the characteristics of the person with whom you least want to spend time:

1.

2.

3.

4.

5.

What did you learn from this exercise? How many of the characteristics are related to attitude? I predict that the person you want to spend time with has characteristics reflective of a positive attitude. Indeed, a positive attitude is a key soft skill people appreciate. Next, list some examples of a positive attitude you exhibit now or that you strive to exhibit. Make a commitment to work through your list until you exhibit each of these characteristics.

List some examples of a positive attitude:

1.

2.

3.

4.

5.

Here are a few examples of a positive attitude that I try to convey:

1. Faith

2. Encouragement

3. Appreciation

4. Sense of humor

5. Resiliency

A positive attitude is important for several reasons: First, **if you are a positive person, people will be drawn to you, and this appeal is a key characteristic of a true leader.** Secondly, your attitude often determines your productivity; most

people are more productive when they have a positive attitude. Plus, a positive attitude helps you handle life's inevitable setbacks. If you ever tried to pull a beach ball underwater, you know that once you let go, the ball immediately races to the surface. Similarly, **your positive attitude gives you buoyancy when life tries to pull you under**. As a Christian, Jesus Christ is the ultimate source of your positive attitude and buoyancy.

Furthermore, **a positive attitude may open opportunities for you** that otherwise you would miss. In my career, I travel frequently, and of course, things don't always go as planned. I recall one flight in particular that was repeatedly delayed and then finally cancelled. The announcement of the cancellation was met with groans from the would-be travelers. We were instructed to get in line at the counter for rebooking. After a long wait, I made it to the counter. I looked at the frazzled person behind the counter and asked her how things were going. She managed a smile and said that things could be better. I told her I realized the cancellation was not her fault, and I appreciated her effort to get me re-booked. She looked a little surprised by my comments. Indeed, several other people had yelled at her even though the flight cancellation was not her fault. She told me to have a seat, and she would call me back when my flights were arranged. Shortly, she called me to the counter and gave me my new ticket. I thanked her and sat down. As I looked at my ticket, I noticed that my row assignment had only one digit. I went back to the counter and asked her if she intentionally upgraded me to first-class. She smiled and said, "Yes." As I returned to my seat, I was reminded of the benefits of a positive attitude. As a Christian, always be gracious and appreciative. You do this not because you might get something, but because you are called to do so.

Leaders must have a positive attitude. As a leader you set the tone for your team. If you are positive, your team will be positive. Essentially, you can inspire or defeat with your attitude. **Effective leaders are able to inspire people and see opportunities where others only see problems; this ability**

requires a positive attitude. Be realistic, but look first for opportunities rather than letting a poor attitude keep you from reaching your potential.

The Bible gives a vivid example of the importance of seeing opportunities rather than problems. God had given the Promised Land to the Israelites. Prior to moving into the land, Moses sent twelve Israelite spies to gather information about the land and the people who lived there. When the spies returned, they reported that the people in the land were strong and the cities were well-secured. This report scared the Israelites. Below is the response of Caleb and some of the other spies.

> ³⁰Then Caleb quieted the people before Moses and said, "We should by all means go up and take possession of it, for we will surely overcome it." ³¹But the men who had gone up with him said, "We are not able to go up against the people, for they are too strong for us." ³²So they gave out to the sons of Israel a bad report of the land which they had spied out, saying, "The land through which we have gone, in spying it out, is a land that devours its inhabitants; and all the people whom we saw in it are men of great size" (Numbers 13:30-32).

Caleb saw an opportunity, and recommended that the Israelites take the Promised Land. However, the other spies saw nothing but problems, and recommended that the Israelites not take the land. Joshua, who also had gone with the spies into the land, stated:

> ⁸If the Lord is pleased with us, then He will bring us into this land and give it to us—a land which flows with milk and honey. ⁹Only do not rebel against the Lord; and do not fear the people of the land, for they will be our prey. Their protection has been removed from them, and the Lord is with us; do not fear them (Numbers 14:8-9).

Joshua and Caleb's comments are insightful for young Christian leaders such as yourself. Caleb saw the opportunity and said "by all means" we should go. Joshua rightly knew that if God was pleased, He would give the land to the Israelites. Joshua cautioned against rebelling against (disobeying) the Lord by failing to take the land that God had given the Israelites. He reminded the Israelites that "The Lord is with us." The point is that God told the Israelites that He would give them the land. They needed to keep their faith, trust God, obey God, and take the opportunity that God gave them.

As a Christian leader, constantly pray to God to know His will. If God tells you to "take the land," you can be confident He will enable you to overcome whatever obstacles seem to be in your way. As you may know, the Israelites did enter the Promised Land. However, of the twelve spies that checked out the land, only Joshua and Caleb were able to enter the Promised Land. God rewarded their faith and leadership.

Maintaining a positive attitude takes a lot of discipline (and faith!), but I assure you it is worth it. Try it for a week and see if you notice a difference in your performance, your relationships, and in your overall outlook on life.

List three specific ways in which you will express a positive attitude this week:

1.

2.

3.

Reflect below on your observations. What did you notice this week?

A positive attitude is easier to maintain if you don't take yourself too seriously. Things will happen that make you look foolish; life is too short to let these things bother you. When I was looking for my first job, I was excited to get an interview for an ideal teaching and research position at a university. I received the itinerary for the interview, which would take place immediately after a professional meeting I was to attend. Because I had the itinerary before I attended the meeting, I made a point of contacting people with whom I would interview. One evening my wife and I went to a restaurant, and in walked one of the people who would interview me. Because he and I had already met (and because I wanted the job), I waved to him. He smiled, waved back, and walked towards me. I smiled, stood up, and extended my hand. Everything was going well until he moved right past me without even noticing I was there. To this day, I don't know who he was going to see, but I know it was not me. So there I was, standing, smiling, and reaching out to shake hands. At this point, I felt like a complete idiot. As I stood there trying to figure out what went wrong, my wife gently encouraged me to sit down. Needless to say, I felt quite foolish. (Had it happened to someone else, it would have been comical, of course.) The point is things like this are going to happen. You can save yourself a lot of stress if you don't take these things too seriously.

Being humble and transparent about your accomplishments is similar to not taking yourself too seriously. **People will respect you more and relate to you better when they see you for who you are. Don't overinflate your accomplishments or try to portray yourself as someone you are not.** Let me use myself as an example. I was elected chairperson of a workshop to be held at a professional scientific meeting. When one of my graduate students learned about my election as chair, he came to me and said, "Oh, Dr. Green! This is a great honor!" Part of me wanted to let him continue to think I was anointed by my peers because of my sheer scientific prowess. However, I have a streak of honesty that often gets in the way of my pride. Thus, I told him not to be too impressed and explained how the anointing actually happened during the chair-selection meeting:

Current chair:	"I am not doing this next year."
Scientist #1:	"I have done this several times, and I am not doing it next year."
Scientist #2:	"Green is new. Let him do it"
Me:	"With that vote of confidence, I humbly accept."

Thus, I was anointed as chair.

The prophet Mica tells us that God requires humility: "He has told you, O man, what is good; And what does the LORD require of you But to do justice, to love kindness, And to walk humbly with your God" (Micah 6:8)? The apostle James tells us that God will reward humility: "Humble yourselves in the presence of the Lord, and He will exalt you" (James 4:10).

The ability to maintain a sense of humor helps you maintain a positive attitude. As I get older, I see more and more how important it is to have a good sense of humor. King Solomon, the wisest man to have ever lived, puts it like this: "A joyful heart is good medicine, But a broken spirit dries up the bones" (Proverbs 17:22). A little well-placed humor often greases the skids of life and helps keep things in perspective. However, remember that **although humor is good, it is no substitute for substance**. People quickly see through a veil of humor if your words and actions lack substance. Sprinkled in the appropriate amounts at the appropriate time, humor can be beneficial. (Please note I am not talking about being snarky or using sarcasm or jokes to demean others. There is no place for this.)

Finally, **have the attitude to go the extra mile**. In other words, do more than is expected of you. Jesus said, "⁴⁰If anyone wants to sue you and take your shirt, let him have your coat also. ⁴¹Whoever forces you to go one mile, go with him two" (Matthew 5:40–41).

Going the extra mile may not seem like much, but seemingly little things often make a big difference. When we were building a house, our builder went the extra mile by stringing our surround-sound wires and by placing some extra flooring in our attic. That may not sound like much, but it would have been a major inconvenience for me to do. Another example comes from the place we get our car serviced: you get a free carwash with each oil change. Again, this may not seem like a huge deal, but it is an extra touch that garners appreciation. The point is this: **People notice, appreciate, and will remember your effort to go the extra mile for them.** These little gestures can make a big difference in the future. (I will discuss this concept further in Chapter 12.)

A Bad Attitude Will Hinder Your Success

Let's switch gears and talk briefly about bad attitudes. When I was in law enforcement, I interacted with many people who displayed a bad attitude. I remember one case in particular, in which a person was causing a disturbance in his neighborhood. We responded to a 911 call and quickly saw that the problem was due entirely to the guy's bad attitude. I explained to him that if his attitude and behavior changed, he could go back home. He agreed and headed home, and we went back on patrol. In about ten minutes we were called back to the same location. Rather than cooling off and leaving his neighbors alone, the guy let his bad attitude continue to drive his actions. This time he went to jail.

A bad attitude may not always land you in jail, but a bad attitude will have negative consequences for you. Attitudes such as arrogance, selfishness, disrespect, jealousy, insecurity, and holding a grudge will greatly diminish your effectiveness. Furthermore, an attitude of doubt can render you completely ineffective if it keeps you from moving forward. **Understand that a bad attitude can undermine a multitude of your great skills and abilities and can limit your success.** Christians should never have a bad attitude, but instead focus on their relationship with Jesus Christ and His grace, blessing, and strength.

Let me share an analogy to show how your bad attitude can limit your success. Consider a plant growing in a flower pot: If you give that plant water, fertilizer, and plenty of sunshine, it should grow. However, if you don't water the plant, it will not grow. Even with plenty of fertilizer and sunshine, the plant won't grow in dry soil. Similarly, you won't grow in the "dry soil" of a bad attitude.

Here is the point: You may be smart, an excellent communicator, and an excellent problem-solver, but your success will be limited if your attitude is bad. If you have a bad attitude, prioritize your effort to improve your attitude.

You can improve your attitude by focusing on the positive aspects of your life and your opportunities instead of focusing on the negative aspects. The Bible is very clear about the importance of focusing on the positives: "Finally, brethren, whatever is true, whatever is honorable, whatever is right, whatever is pure, whatever is lovely, whatever is of good repute, if there is any excellence and if anything worthy of praise, dwell on these things" (Philippians 4:8).

Don't dwell on your mistakes, losses, and failures, but focus on what you have and what you can achieve. God can move you past setbacks. Some people mistakenly think that God keeps track of every mistake that he or she has ever made, and that he or she can never overcome failure or mistakes. This thinking is not Biblical. **God will forgive you and will forget your sins when you confess and repent. Although there may be very real consequences to deal with, God will not hold your mistakes against you.** God tells us that, "I, even I, am the one who wipes out your transgressions for My own sake, And I will not remember your sins" (Isaiah 43:25). Furthermore, Paul assures Christians that: "Therefore there is now no condemnation for those who are in Christ Jesus" (Romans 8:1). Receive the grace of Jesus Christ, and move past your mistakes, losses, and failures. (We will discuss mistakes in more detail in Chapter 12.)

Additionally, if you want to improve your attitude, don't make negative comments. I have often heard people say, "I will never learn chemistry," or "I will never get a good job." Do not speak negatively about yourself. The Bible cautions about losing confidence: "Therefore, do not throw away your confidence, which has a great reward" (Hebrews 10:35).

Furthermore, don't dwell on negative emotions. Strive to see opportunities rather than obstacles. See other people as helping you, not holding you back. See yourself as succeeding rather than failing. Finally, if you want to improve your attitude, find some positive, encouraging people to spend time with. (I will discuss this strategy further in the "Your Inner Circle" section.)

Also understand that your attitude influences how you think. My experience is that **many people waste valuable time and energy, and create unnecessary stress for themselves, by worrying about things they need not worry about.** The apostle Paul realized how easily we can worry and get discouraged. He tells us in Philippians 4:6–7 that we should, "6Be anxious for nothing, but in everything by prayer and supplication with thanksgiving let your requests be made known to God.7And the peace of God, which surpasses all understanding, will guard your hearts and your minds in Christ Jesus." These verses have been very powerful in my life, and they can help you, too, when facing challenges. For example, rather than worrying about a chemistry test, pray, "Father God, You said You would help me. I am worried about this test. Please guide my studying and give me wisdom. Empower me to do my best on this test." Notice that the prayer includes "studying!" You must work hard to learn the material, as well as ask God help you as you prepare and take the test.

Have you ever dreaded something (such as a meeting, a class, a test, or a difficult conversation) only to realize afterward that it was not so bad, or that you did much better than expected? Likely you made up a very negative scenario focusing on everything that could go wrong. You repeatedly replayed that scenario in your mind, thereby stressing and worrying until the situation passed. The outcome was likely not nearly as bad as you had imagined.

It seems some people are not happy unless they can worry about something and develop a bad attitude, even if they have to make it up. The next time you are feeling worried, stressed, or anxious, realistically assess your thinking. You might find that you are artificially creating stress because you are telling yourself a very negative story. Here's a novel solution: Tell yourself a positive story instead of a negative one.

You can also experience less stress and worry by addressing the worrisome situation sooner rather than later. For example, I once dreaded the need to have a very unpleasant conversation with someone. I had put the conversation off for a week. I considered putting the conversation off until the following Monday. However, rather than waiting until Monday and having to worry about the conversation all weekend, I talked to the person on Friday. I learned two important points from this situation: First, the actual conversation was not nearly as bad as I had assumed; I should not have wasted so much time and energy worrying. Second, by having the conversation on Friday, I was able to enjoy my weekend. The best way to avoid unnecessary stress and worry is to engage in your perceived unpleasant situation sooner rather than later. Doing so will save you a lot of stress. In this example, I felt the Holy Spirit guiding me to have the conversation on Friday rather than on Monday. Ask God, and He tell you when the time is right for the conversation.

As you can see, creating and dwelling on a worst-case scenario used to be a common occurrence for me, but I have made great progress in this area. In a conversation with my mentor, I was lamenting an issue with which I was struggling. My mentor asked a question that seemed quite random at the time, "What were you worried about this time last year?" I thought for a while and told her I did not remember. She asked, "What about three months ago?" A few things came to mind, but not many. She then asked about last week. Again, I had an item or two on my list of historical worries, but not many. Then she taught me the lesson: I often spent a lot of time worrying about things, and rarely should I have worried as much as I did. She said that most things that seem so ominous at the time really are not that bad. Later, you may not even remember things you stressed over. Although you certainly should take your challenges seriously, don't invest too much time, energy, and stress on them. In the months since she taught me this lesson, I have been able to decrease my stress and increase my contentment. You can experience the same results if you stop dwelling on negative thoughts. (Remember Philippians 4:6–7.)

Finally, **don't let a negative attitude influence how you respond to something you read or hear**. I once received from a staff member an e-mail that made me mad (more accurately, I chose to get mad after I read it). I went to her office and told her about the many shortcomings of her e-mail, and that I did not like her tone. She responded with a very surprised look on her face. Later, she said she could see how I could interpret her e-mail as I had. She further explained that she did not intend it to be negative. I apologized after hearing her explanation. Her message was clear indeed. However, I chose to have a bad attitude and negatively interpret the e-mail. The learning point here is that I got mad and had a stern, unpleasant conversation that could have been avoided had I not read the e-mail with a bad attitude. I have seen countless people make this same mistake. The solution is simple: **Don't create negativity. If you are going to make an assumption, assume the best rather than the worst.**

List below five characteristics of a bad attitude that you exhibit. Make a commitment to work through your list until none remain. Ask a close friend for input; he or she may see things that you don't.

1.

2.

3.

4.

5.

I will end this section on bad attitude with a few words of caution: **Don't get caught up in a "that's not fair" attitude.** For a long time, I thought many of my experiences were not fair. It was not fair that I had to work on my uncle's farm when my friends went fishing. It was not fair that my chemistry lab partner did not do enough work. It was not fair that someone backed into my car and drove off without leaving a note. And the list goes on and on.

I finally realized I was wasting time stressing over injustices that did not really exist, and I was wasting effort trying to change things beyond my control. Do what I did: Develop the attitude that life sometimes is not going to be fair and move on. If you let yourself believe that life should be fair, you will be disappointed constantly, which could give you a bad attitude.

Let's look more deeply at "That's not fair." Life is not fair in terms of the grace we receive from God. The apostle Paul puts it this way: "But by the grace of God I am what I am, and His grace toward me did not prove vain; but I labored even more than all of them, yet not I, but the grace of God with me" (1 Corinthians 15:10).

Paul knows what he is talking about. Before he was known as the apostle Paul, he was Saul of Tarsus, and he persecuted many Christians because of their faith. Frankly, he deserved to be punished for what he did to Christians. However, God forgave Paul and used him mightily. It is not fair that God forgave Paul, used him in building the early church, and also used him to write many books in the New Testament. Considering all the mistakes I have made, it is not fair that Jesus died for the forgiveness of my sins and that He has a great plan for my life. Do not worry about the fact that you do not deserve God's grace or the abundant life that He has for you; no one deserves it. His grace is available to you; all you have to do is ask. Christians are very fortunate that God is "not fair."

Your Inner Circle

At the beginning of this chapter, I asked you to list the characteristics of people you do and do not like to spend time with. Let's explore this concept more deeply here. I want to make the point that you are influenced by the attitude of your friends. We read in Proverbs that, "The righteous is a guide to his neighbor, But the way of the wicked leads them astray." (Proverbs 12:26). In some translations, the term "friend" is used instead of neighbor. You likely have lots of friends, but only a few friends who are really close to you. Your closest friends are in your "inner circle." **Your inner circle should include only those people who inspire, encourage, and support you.**

Jesus had twelve disciples, but only three were in His inner circle. He traveled with the twelve, but we see in Scripture that Jesus often was alone with His inner circle. For example, we read in Mark 5:37, "And He allowed no one to accompany Him, except Peter and James and John the brother of James." Jesus clearly modeled that you should have an inner circle comprised of your most-trusted friends. Jesus said of Peter: "I also say to you that you are Peter, and upon this rock I will build My church; and the gates of Hades will not overpower it" (Matthew 16:18). It is widely known that John is referred to as the disciple whom Jesus loved. In John 19:26 we read: "When Jesus saw his mother and the disciple whom he loved standing nearby, he said to his mother, "Woman, behold, your son!" The Bible does not tell us much about James, but you can be sure that Jesus had a very good reason for including James in His inner circle.

I have seen several young people who were held back by the attitudes and actions of people in their inner circle. Often, these young people feel awkward when they achieve more than their friends, so sometimes they don't achieve what they otherwise could. And when they do achieve something, their friends make fun of them for doing well. I also have known students who have not done their best work because they hung out with friends who did not work hard or who were content with just getting by; they simply developed the bad attitude of their friends. If you are surrounded by friends like this, don't let them into your inner circle and influence negatively your attitude. Of course you can still be friends, but I encourage you to find new friends for your inner circle.

I realize that finding new friends can be difficult, and that you may not want to distance yourself from some of your close friends. However, consider the fact that if you surround yourself with people who have no goals or who have a bad attitude, soon you will think and act like them, which will hinder your success. Several years ago, I had a friend who had a very negative attitude. She often would say, "I can never get it right." I tried hard to encourage her and help her improve her attitude. However, her attitude never improved. And one day, when I was working on a task, I said out loud, "I can never get this right." I usually am a very positive person, so this statement was a complete surprise to me. Frankly, I was shocked when I said it. If you spend a lot of time with people who have a bad attitude, that attitude will have a negative impact on you.

I have worked with some people who always complain, speak negatively about nearly everything, and who will point out every reason why things will go wrong. I usually feel worse after I talk to these people. I worked with these people and could not completely ignore them, but I did not let them in my inner circle because I did not want to hear their constant negativity. On the other hand, I have worked with people and have friends who are always positive, inspiring, and encouraging. These people see potential success instead of seeing every reason something might fail. I look forward to spending time with these people, and I let them in my inner circle. I get energized and encouraged when I talk to them. Do yourself a favor, and **fill your inner circle with people who will lift you up rather than bring you down.** These people will contribute to your success. Below is a list of characteristics that people in your inner circle should have:

1. Strong Christian faith

2. Positive attitude

3. Goals, ambitions, and a strong work ethic

4. Encouraging attitude

5. Energizing personality

6. Ability to inspire you to achieve

7. Self-confidence to celebrate your successes

You can positively influence those around you. The apostle Paul says: "[12]Let no one look down on your youthfulness, but rather in speech, conduct, love, faith and purity, show yourself an example of those who believe (1 Timothy 4:12). Being a Christian example can be tough, but God will equip you to be His example if you allow Him to live in and through you.

Additionally, when you see someone sinning you can encourage him or her to confess, turn from the sin, and seek God's forgiveness. Pray with and for the person and ask God to work powerfully in his or her life. If the person has not received his or her salvation, share the information in the "Receive Salvation" section of this book. Finally, remember that you (and I) also sin and need God's grace. Therefore, do not throw a judgmental stone at someone who is sinning.

Key points from Chapter 2:

1. God's peace, grace, and hope should give all Christians a positive attitude.

2. People generally are more productive when they have a positive attitude.

3. God can empower you to control your attitude, even if you can't control your circumstances.

4. Don't endure unnecessary stress and anxiety by creating worst-case scenarios and then playing them over in your mind.

5. God does not keep track of your mistakes when you ask for His forgiveness, and you should not keep track either.

6. If you are worried about a situation, ask God to show you the right time to address it.

7. A positive attitude provides emotional buoyancy.

8. A positive attitude will give you more opportunities than will a negative attitude.

9. Effective leaders see opportunities where others see problems.

10. Maintain a sense of humor.

11. Have the attitude to go the extra mile and exceed expectations.

12. A negative attitude can limit your success even if you have many excellent skills and abilities.

13. Surround yourself with people who inspire, encourage, and support you.

14. Be a Godly example to those around you.

15. Encourage confession and repentance, but don't be judgemental.

Please reflect on what you learned in this chapter and answer the following questions:

1. In your own words, explain what it means to be positive.

2. Why is it important to be positive?

3. What are the three most significant things you learned from this chapter?

4. List three specific things you will work on to be positive.

5. What benefit will you experience by following through on the items listed in Question 4?

Chapter 3: Balance Your Life and Keep Learning

Take a minute and think about what is really important to you. Hopefully, you are thinking about different areas of your life: faith, family, friends, goals, school, work, volunteering, and so on. Life balance refers to the ability to focus effort and energy in each important area in your life rather than focusing on only one or two areas. **Generally, you are more successful and happier when your life is in balance.**

Although you may have several important areas in your life, you may focus too much on one or two areas. In the short term, this imbalanced focus may be acceptable. However, in the longer term, imbalance can lead to losing very important things in your life: your closeness with Jesus Christ, family, friends, and health. Furthermore, if your life is not balanced, you likely cannot continue to be productive very long. Finally, realize that if your life is out of balance, the effects likely are felt by those people you care about the most.

A Balancing Act

I think the key to understanding why people get out of balance is to consider how people define success. I used to define success solely as success at work. During this time my health suffered, and I was not spending quality time with my wife. Success at work is good, but not at the expense of other areas of your life, such as family, friends, and your health. Don't sacrifice life balance pursuing workplace success.

It's easy for Christians to get caught up in the world's definition of success, and to chase everything the world has to offer. Soon we can find our lives out of balance. But we don't have to live this way. Indeed, Paul warns us against chasing the world's trappings: "And do not be conformed to this world, but be transformed by the renewing of your mind, so that you may prove what the will of God is, that which is good and acceptable and perfect" (Romans 12:2). Furthermore, John tells us that, "The world is passing away, and also its lusts; but the one who does the will of God lives forever" (1 John 2:17).

As a Christian, your personal relationship with Jesus Christ is your first priority. However, some times the drive for worldly success and material things gets in the way. Jesus warns about the drive for worldly desires in the Gospel of Mark: "But the worries of the world, and the deceitfulness of riches, and the desires for other things enter in and choke the word, and it becomes unfruitful" (Mark 4:19). The phrase "choke the word" means that competing priorities can interfere with your pursuit of God and His plan for your life. When this interference occurs, your life is out of balance. Describe in the space below what "living a successful life" means to you:

Please complete the following exercise to determine how balanced your life is. I have listed several areas of potential importance in your life in Table 1. (Please feel free to edit.) For each area in Table 1, rank its importance to you: Very Important, Average Importance, Low Importance, or Not Important. At this point in your life, everything may seem important. However, you must realize that rarely will you have time to do everything. Thus, know what is most important and spend your time on the truly important things in your life.

Next, estimate the amount of time you spend currently in each area. Estimate time spent as: Too Much, Just About Right, or Not Enough. Keep in mind that merely spending time in an area does not necessarily mean it is important to you. This exercise can help you determine if you are investing your time in areas of your life that are meaningful and that will benefit your future. (We will talk more about goal setting and prioritization in Chapters 9 and 10.)

To see how much time you actually spend in each area, keep track of time spent in each area for the next three or four weeks. You don't need to keep track of every minute, but you must have enough information to make a valid assessment of how you spend your time. Keeping track of your time in thirty-minute increments should be adequate. Use this information to fill in the "Actual" time spent on each activity.

In the "Assessment" section, comment on how you spent your time in each area. Did you spend the most time on the "Very Important" areas of your life and the least amount on the "Not Important" areas? Did your results surprise you? I have seen students define areas as important, and then discover that they did not spend much time on that area. This discrepancy suggests that life may be out of balance, which often causes stress and creates guilty feelings. The good news is that you can rebalance your life, and doing so will make you feel better.

Develop an "Action Plan" based on your assessment. For example, you may have listed "Family" as "Very Important," but discovered you did not spend much time with your family. This imbalance may be stressful or cause you to feel guilty. Your Action Plan would be to spend more time with your family. Be sure to put specific activities in your plan. You might take your younger sister to a movie or have a meal with your family. Again, realize that the amount of time spent does not tell the whole story; focus your action plan on impactful activities, not just on spending time.

After you work your action plan for a few weeks, repeat the exercise and answer the following questions:

1. Did your original estimate of importance and "Time Spent" on the categories match the reality of how you actually spent your time?

2. If not, have you made real changes to the way that you spend your time?

3. Are you investing your time in areas that will prepare you for your future, or are you just spending time on things that may not matter in the future?

4. Do you feel that you have more peace and contentment as you balance your life?

5. What is the most important thing you learned from this exercise?

Table 1: Life Balance Worksheet

Area	Importance	Estimated time spent	Actual time spent	Assessment	Action Plan
Exercise					
Family					
Friends					
Goals					
Hobbies					
Relationship with Jesus					
School					
Sleep					
Social media/ gaming					
Sports					
Time alone					
Volunteering					
Work					

Live and Learn

In addition to keeping your life balanced, commit to life-long learning if you want to be successful. Have you ever thought about the fact that graduation ceremonies are referred to as "commencement" ceremonies? This suggests that things are starting rather than ending. When I graduated from college with my BS degree, I felt I knew less than I did when I started college. At first, this feeling surprised me. However, upon reflection, I realized that I had received an excellent education. I learned a lot as a student, but I also learned that I still had a lot to learn. When I finished my PhD program, I had a pretty good understanding of a lot of things; however, as I began my career, I found I still had a lot to learn. I've been out of graduate school for more years than I care to count, and I continue learning. **Commitment to lifelong learning is critical to your continual progress and is a key characteristic of leaders who conquer increasingly difficult challenges.**

Not only will future challenges be difficult, but they may not even exist today. A colleague of mine tells a story that you may not believe. When he was in high school, a speaker told students in his class that they would be working in careers and facing challenges that currently didn't exist. My colleague said he did not believe the speaker at the time, but he now knows the speaker was correct. Consider this example: Careers in social media that exist today did not exist a few short years ago. **You are preparing to address issues and work in a career that currently doesn't exist.** Therefore, embrace lifelong learning.

The importance of lifelong learning is clearly described by King Solomon in Proverbs. Solomon is widely known as the wisest man who ever lived, and his wisdom came from God. Solomon says that a wise and prudent person will "increase in learning," "be still wiser," and "seek knowledge." You can experience the same increase if you commit to lifelong learning:

- "A wise man will hear and increase in learning, and a man of understanding will acquire wise counsel" (Proverbs 1:5).
- "Give instruction to a wise man and he will be still wiser, teach a righteous man and he will increase his learning" (Proverbs 9:9).
- "The mind of the prudent acquires knowledge, and the ear of the wise seeks knowledge" (Proverbs 18:15).

Pray that God makes you wise and prudent. The apostle James says: "But if any of you lacks wisdom, let him ask of God, who gives to all generously and without reproach, and it will be given to him" (James 1:5).

A mentor helped me understand the importance of lifelong learning. I asked him what advice he had for me as I began my career. I still remember his words as if the conversation took place this morning: "No one cares what you know about nitrogen cycling (the topic of my graduate research). What is important are the skills you have learned that you can apply to other research topics." I was shocked to hear what he said. I had spent six years working a ridiculous number of hours reading research papers, conducting my own nitrogen cycling research experiments, presenting data at professional meetings, and publishing manuscripts on my nitrogen cycling research. I had pulled all-nighters and worked on weekends, evenings, and holidays. I had literally poured my life into my research on nitrogen. And nobody cares about what I know about nitrogen? Well, that was indeed what I heard, but that was not what he said.

My mentor was telling me that my education was not over when graduate school ended, but was, in fact, beginning. I could not rely solely on what I learned in the past, but I needed to keep learning and leverage my skills to increase my ability to solve new problems. In short, I had to commit to lifelong learning. His advice has proven to be absolutely correct.

Lifelong learning requires you to improve existing skills and also develop new skills. One of the most significant lifelong learning moments in my leadership life came in 1998, three years into my faculty career. I was doing well securing several research grants, and I had earned a teaching award. However, I realized that to reach my goals, I needed to improve my leadership and soft skills. Don't miss this point: I had to improve my leadership and soft skills in addition to my technical skills to progress in my career. The same is true for you.

Certainly, lifelong learning seems obvious to me now, but you must make a conscious effort to learn. Recognize this fact and **look for and take advantage of opportunities to learn, and engage in activities that stretch you**. If you are complacent or if you merely are not looking for the chance to learn, excellent opportunities will pass you by. Although you may not be disadvantaged directly, you certainly will lose the chance to grow.

Consider this sports analogy: Entire games often are won or lost in very brief moments. Winners in sports are those who gain an advantage, often only for a brief time. For example, how many times have you seen a basketball team go on a "ten-two run" in five minutes and then win the game by seven or eight points? The victory goes back to that brief five-minute period when they gained an advantage.

You gain a similar advantage in life by engaging in the right opportunities. Deliberately look for and take advantage of growth opportunities. These opportunities include reading and applying the concepts in this book. Other opportunities include taking a leadership position in an organization at school, leading a Bible study, or seeking a mentor to give you advice. **Realize that engaging in a single opportunity can set you on an entirely different trajectory for your life.** I wish I would have better understood this concept when I was younger. Always look for growth opportunities, especially if the opportunity will stretch you.

Let me share an example to illustrate the impact of a single opportunity. I advised a leadership development program for several years. Although the program greatly enhanced the professional development of dozens of young people, the impact on one young man in particular stands out. Despite the fact that his apparent leadership ability was far behind his peers, this young man took a risk and applied for admission to the program. Luckily, he was selected. Initially, he was very shy and possessed few discernable leadership or soft skills. The leadership program gave him the opportunity to develop his academic, leadership, and soft skills. He worked hard and became one the most accomplished students in the program. He earned the respect of his peers and graduated from college. Furthermore, he continued his education and earned a master's degree.

The student set aside his doubt and took a risk. He took advantage of an opportunity, and that opportunity changed the trajectory of his entire life.

Key points from Chapter 3:

1. Success in life includes balancing several areas of your life.

2. Don't let the trapping of life choke out God's plan for your life.

3. Spend time in each area of importance in your life.

4. You are preparing to work in a career and to solve problems that don't exist now.

5. The skills you need to succeed go way beyond the technical skills of your chosen field.

6. Engage in activities that stretch you.

7. Take advantage of every opportunity to learn.

8. Wise people continue to learn.

9. God will give you wisdom if you ask Him.

Please reflect on what you learned in this chapter and answer the following questions:

1. In your own words, explain what it means to balance your life and keep learning.

2. Why is it important to commit to balance and lifelong learning?

3. What are the three most significant things you learned from this chapter?

4. List three specific things you will work on to commit to lifelong learning.

5. What benefit will you experience by following through on the items listed in Question 4?

Chapter 4: Keep Things in Context

Context refers to a frame of reference. As a Christian, your frame of reference is your identity in Christ. The following verses should guide your thinking and enable you to live an abundant and successful life:

- "I will give thanks to You, for I am fearfully and wonderfully made; Wonderful are Your works, And my soul knows it very well" (Psalm 139:14).
- "The angel of the LORD encamps around those who fear Him, And rescues them" (Psalm 34:7).
- "But as many as received Him, to them He gave the right to become children of God, even to those who believe in His name" (John 1:12).
- "Therefore let us draw near with confidence to the throne of grace, so that we may receive mercy and find grace to help in time of need" (Hebrews 4:16).
- "Do not fear, for I am with you; Do not anxiously look about you, for I am your God. I will strengthen you, surely I will help you, Surely I will uphold you with My righteous right hand" (Isaiah 41:10).
- "'For I know the plans that I have for you,' declares the Lord, 'plans for welfare and not for calamity to give you a future and a hope'" (Jeremiah 29:11).

- "The LORD your God is in your midst, A victorious warrior. He will exult over you with joy, He will be quiet in His love, He will rejoice over you with shouts of joy" (Zephaniah 3:17).
- For we are his workmanship, created in Christ Jesus for good works, which God prepared beforehand, that we should walk in them" (Ephesians 2:10).

Your identity in Christ comes with lots of perks! God knew what He was doing when He created you; you are fearfully and wonderfully made. In fact, you are a child of God. Angels encamp around you. God has a plan for your life. God delights in you and rejoices over you. You have been prepared for good works. You can be confident that God will give you mercy, grace, help, and strength. I encourage you to read these verses every day and be confident in your identity in Christ and the tremendous love He has for you.

To be successful, to enjoy life, and to recover from setbacks, you must understand that God controls every aspect of your life. Nothing "just happens" to Christians. Let me share an example of how God showed this principle to me. When I was in graduate school, I was engaged to be married. My fiancé and I were living 500 miles apart, and, frankly, we were having some rough telephone conversations. We needed to see each other, so I took off a few days of work to visit her and attend an event.

However, we decided to skip the event and go to our hometown. We stopped by my parents' house, but no one was home. Soon, my great-aunt knocked on the door. I invited her in, and she said, "You don't know, do you?" I asked, "Know what?" She said, "Cary, your Dad had a heart attack." I looked at my fiancé and said, "Let's go to the hospital." My great-aunt then said, "Cary, he died." I was shocked. I had talked to my Dad just a few days earlier, and he was fine. He recently had a medical check-up and was fine. However, he had a massive heart attack that morning and died; he was only forty-nine. As I was trying to process the news, my Mom returned from the hospital.

You may be wondering how this shows that God is in control of every aspect of my life. Here's how: Rather than being 500 miles away, I was sitting on my Mom's couch when she came home from the hospital. I was able to comfort her immediately rather than having to make an 8-hour drive.

I had no idea my Dad was going to die. I was totally oblivious to what God was doing, but He orchestrated circumstances to get me where I needed to be at the exact moment I needed to be there. That experience took place more than twenty-five years ago, and I still thank God every single day for loving me enough to orchestrate that trip and ask Him to continue to guide me. Read this story again. What a remarkable God we serve.

Keep Your Eyes on the Prize

Context also provides motivation for your activities and keeps you focused on your priorities. You can easily get caught up in the little details of what you are doing and lose the overall context of your bigger goals or priorities. When this happens, you often get frustrated and want to give up. **You can save yourself a lot of frustration by keeping things in context.** In other words, **think of your current activities in terms of your overall goals.**

When I was an assistant professor, my main goal was to attain tenure and be promoted to the rank of professor. These are two milestones of advancement in a career in higher education; obtaining these goals would set me up for additional opportunities that otherwise would be unattainable. One day I found myself especially frustrated with the hours I spent working on statistical analyses. I thought about how much I disliked statistics and asked myself the question, "Is this what my career is about....doing statistics all day?" Well, as I reflected on this rhetorical question, the answer came to me quite clearly: "No!" I had lost the context of what I was doing. I was focusing on a boring activity I did not particularly like, and that focus was consuming a lot of my energy. My attitude was bad, and I certainly was not productive.

My attitude and productivity improved dramatically when I regained the proper context: I was statistically analyzing data so that I could publish my research. The resultant publication was part of the requirements for attaining promotion and tenure. So when I focused on the context of getting promotion and tenure, a vitally important goal for me, I saw statistics for what it was—a necessary step in my march toward my goal. Needless to say, my attitude changed. I was not a big fan of statistics, but I was happy to do the analyses to allow me to get publications and achieve my goal. The moral to the story is **don't lose the context of what you are doing by focusing only on the little details. Keep your eye on your bigger goals.** The apostle Paul puts it this way: "I press on toward the goal for the prize of the upward call of God in Christ Jesus" Philippians 3:14).

Let me share an example that may resonate with students: I have talked to countless students who were burning out and getting frustrated with something such as a chemistry test, an English paper, or a class project. I asked the student why he wanted to go to college. He replied that he wanted to obtain a degree and gain skills that would help him secure a good job and set him up for a successful life. I asked him if he needed to graduate from college or just attend to meet these goals. He agreed that he needed to graduate. I asked him if the class he struggled with was required for his degree. He confirmed that it was. (Some students would be catching on at this point.) So then I asked him to look at the test (or paper or project) in the context of a necessary step towards achieving his goal of a better chance at having a successful life via obtaining a college degree. In other words, keep the proper context; keep the "big picture" in mind.

Describe below some of your current activities that seem especially stressful or monotonous. Can you see these activities as part of a bigger goal?

Down But Not Out

Context also is important in terms of daily trials and tribulations. I have not succeeded at everything I attempted, and I doubt that you will either. Therefore, it is important to understand that **your life is not defined by one bad grade on a test or in a class, by one failed project, by one missed opportunity, by one loss at a competition, or by one poor performance on the job.** When you come up short, keep moving forward and strive for improvement. Recall the example of my poor grade in chemistry. I easily could have given up, but I kept the setback in context and tried again. I succeeded the second time and also in subsequent classes; I even tutored a student in the graduate course I took. Had I seen the chemistry class as indicative of my ability, I would have given up. Learn from my experience and **don't let a single setback escalate into an obstacle for future growth.** Keep it in the right context and move ahead.

Let's explore this concept a little further. Recall that context is a frame of reference. You will face occasional losses, shortcomings, and setbacks: You may not make the varsity squad, get the position you wanted in an organization, win the competition, get into the university you always wanted to attend, land your dream job, or get the promotion you wanted. When this setback happens, you may choose to focus on what you did not get, what you lost, or on your mistakes. If you choose to focus on these setbacks, you are destined for perpetual frustration, stress, and disappointment. This stress and frustration will take a toll on your attitude and confidence and likely will cause you to doubt your abilities, which, in turn, will make it difficult for you to move forward. In other words, if you focus on your mistakes, you may be afraid to move ahead. Your growth and progress will be greatly diminished if you never try again.

Recall that my grades my first semester in college nearly caused me to quit school. But I did not give up. I was not sure I would succeed in college, but I made up my mind that I would not give up without trying again. I learned to rely on God and to be a better student. I succeeded in my classes the second time. I went on to be successful as a professor and university administrator. God moved me beyond my setback, and He will move you beyond your setbacks.

Remember what the apostle Paul tells us: "And we know that God causes all things to work together for good to those who love God, to those who are called according to His purpose" (Romans 8:28). I would not have had the motivation to call out to God and to develop the skills I needed to succeed in college had I not struggled so much during my freshman year. The grade that almost caused me to quit school actually set me up for success. If you would have told me after that first semester that I would eventually get a PhD and teach at a university, I would have laughed in your face. I did not understand Romans 8:28 at that point in my life.

If you choose to keep your setbacks in the proper context, and embrace Romans 8:28, you can learn from your setbacks without being defined by them. I challenge you to focus on what you have and what you can do rather than on what you lost or what you can't do. **Don't be defined by what knocks you down; be defined by what you go on to accomplish.**

Answer the following questions to describe an example of receiving a "bad grade" or similar setback in your life:

1. How long ago was it?

2. Were you able to rise above it?

3.   Did you think you would rise above it?

4.   What did you learn that you can apply the next time you face a setback?

5.   Ask your mentor to tell you about a time when he overcame a setback.

I sometimes tell young people that they should be a cannon ball rather than a ping-pong ball. When a cannon ball encounters an obstacle, it has the momentum to blast through and keep going. A ping-pong ball will simply bounce off an obstacle. Recognize that you will encounter many obstacles in your lifetime. Develop a cannon ball mentality and push through every obstacle you encounter. Pray for God's strength and trust Him to guide you past your obstacles.

Key points from Chapter 4:

1.   Your identity in Christ sets the context for your life.

2.   Context provides the overall motivation for what you do.

3.   Think of your current activities in terms of your overall goals.

4.   Life is not defined by one bad event.

5.   Don't be defined by what knocks you down; be defined by what you go on to accomplish.

6.   God can use your setbacks to prepare you for a great future.

Please reflect on what you learned in this chapter and answer the following questions.

1. In your own words, explain what it means to keep things in context.

2. Why is it important to keep things in context?

3. What are the three most significant points you learned from this chapter?

4. List two or three specific things you will work on to keep things in context.

5. What benefit will you experience by following through on the items listed in Question 4?

Part II: Relationships

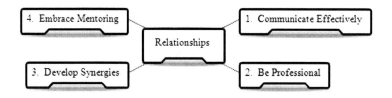

4. Embrace Mentoring

1. Communicate Effectively

Relationships

3. Develop Synergies

2. Be Professional

Jesus once was asked what the most important commandment was: "And He said to him, 'YOU SHALL LOVE THE LORD YOUR GOD WITH ALL YOUR HEART, AND WITH ALL YOUR SOUL, AND WITH ALL YOUR MIND. [38]This is the great and foremost commandment. [39]The second is like it, YOU SHALL LOVE YOUR NEIGHBOR AS YOUR-SELF'" (Matthew 22:37-39). As Christians, our relationship with God is our highest priority, and our relationships with others is our next highest priority.

While in graduate school, I mentioned to a friend that someday I wanted to be a department head at a university. He said he thought I would be a good department head and that I had the "people skills" to be a good leader. I respected my friend because he had been successful in business before taking a job at the university, but his comment did not resonate in my narrow mind. In fact, my reaction was that I will succeed because I am a good scientist, soon to have a PhD. I thought people skills were overrated and that you only needed them if you were not very competent. Frankly, I was naïve thinking that way. Fortunately, I learned that my friend was exactly right: People skills are critical to your success.

To succeed, you must be competent, and you also must be able to get along with people—both are important. Since that conversation twenty-five years ago, I have worked with some very gifted scientists who had the people skills of a rabid pit bull. They were smart, but they could not get along with others. Conversely, I have worked with some absolutely wonderful people who were not very competent. They were nice, but they could not adequately perform their job duties. Fortunately, these two extremes are not prevalent. I have had the pleasure to work with countless individuals who excelled at their jobs and also were great people with whom to work. Your goal should be to **excel in the competence of your chosen field and also create and maintain relationships.** Otherwise, your success will be hindered.

Furthermore, building relationships will help you develop a network of friends and contacts. **Networking often provides leads for jobs and resources for solving problems, both of which can greatly enhance your success.** I have helped several friends get jobs by alerting them of opportunities or writing reference letters, and they have done the same for me. I also have called on my network to help me solve a problem that I could not solve. Perhaps you have heard the expression, "It's not what you know but who you know that is important." Networking is about who you know.

Finally, realize that **the overall quality of your life often mirrors the quality of your relationships.** If you are not as happy, productive, or as fulfilled as you want to be, take an inventory of your relationships. Invest time in your relationships that are not as strong as they could be. Surround yourself with people who inspire, encourage, and support you. And be sure that you are a positive influence on your friends. **Ultimately, it is our relationships with Jesus Christ and those He brings into our lives that truly matter.**

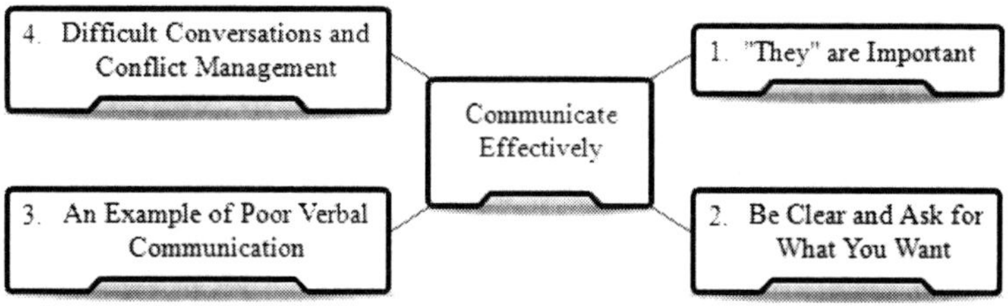
4. Difficult Conversations and Conflict Management
Communicate Effectively
1. "They" are Important
3. An Example of Poor Verbal Communication
2. Be Clear and Ask for What You Want

Chapter 5: Communicate Effectively

A person who has great vision and ideas but can't communicate them is no different from someone who does not have great vision and ideas. The ability to communicate effectively is absolutely essential for your success.

Communication includes typical activities such as speaking, writing, and listening. However, effective communication requires much more. **To communicate effectively, be clear in your content, context, and intent.** Content, of course, is the message you communicate to someone. Context helps the person understand the background of your message, and intent lets the person know the reason for your communication. For example, I may send an e-mail to one of my mentees: "Dear John: The last time we talked, we discussed that you have a major project due in three weeks (context). I am writing to see if you have developed the timeline for your project (intent)." This approach is more effective than e-mailing, "Hey man, got your timeline done?" I commonly get e-mail from young people that is closer to "Hey man," which is poor communication. Whether speaking or writing, be sure your audience understands the context and intent of your communication. Otherwise, you will have to spend extra time to clarify later.

"They" are Important

There is a saying in education: "Students don't care what you know until they know that you care." I believe the same principle applies to communication. **Communicate authenticity and genuine concern for the people to whom you are speaking**. Try to understand the perspective of the people to whom you communicate. And **communicate so that the other person can understand and benefit**; in other words, **focus on her not yourself**. The apostle Paul puts it like this: "Do nothing from selfishness or empty conceit, but with humility of mind regard one another as more important than yourselves" (Philippians 2:3).

I struggled in this area early in my career. I remember one particular venue in which a colleague and I were speaking on environmental issues to a large audience. The background of individuals in the audience was quite varied, and their goal was to learn something that would make them more effective in their jobs. However, rather than developing a message that would be of value to them, I spoke to impress them with what I knew. Looking back, I was motivated by arrogance rather than by concern for the audience. Although I succeeded in giving a complicated presentation, I failed miserably in providing information that was of practical value. I wanted to impress them, but I did not understand that the key to impressing them was giving them information they could use. Here is my point: Whether communicating with one person or one hundred, understand the perspective of your audience and craft your message for their understanding and benefit.

Effective communicators are great listeners. Listening requires that you pay attention to the conversation at hand and that you don't let your mind wander. **Great listeners ask great questions.** Listening shows that you care. I also notice that I hear and retain more when I listen intently.

We often listen with the objectives of making comments or solving problems. These objectives can be admirable, but often, the person who is speaking simply wants to be heard. In other words, the purpose of a conversation may be to allow him to work through and express his ideas. He may not need your opinion; if he does, he will ask. The apostle James tells us: "This you know, my beloved brethren. But everyone must be quick to hear, slow to speak and slow to anger" (James 1:19).

Early in our marriage, my wife would come home from work and share her experiences of the day. I often made quick comments or gave her solutions to perceived issues. I soon learned that she did not need all of my comments. She simply wanted to talk. She would ask for my input sometimes, but not as often as I gave it. **Don't underestimate the value of simply letting someone talk to you while he or she has your undivided attention and without your interruption.**

Effective communicators listen without interrupting. Please understand that finishing someone's sentence is an interruption. When you interrupt someone you send the message that what he has to say is not important. Taken to the extreme, he can think you are rude and/or that he is not important to you.

Furthermore, when you interrupt, you have not heard everything that the other person is trying to say. Thus, you may say something foolish. We read in the Proverbs: "He who gives an answer before he hears, It is folly and shame to him" (Proverbs 18:13).

Watch your nonverbal communication when you listen. Perhaps you have experienced speaking to someone who is looking around, drumming his fingers on the table, texting, sighing often, and so on. What does this nonverbal communication indicate? It clearly sends the message that he is not really interested in what you have to say. Be aware of your body language and refrain from sending the wrong message.

Make a deliberate effort to watch your nonverbal communication and that of others over the next few days. Record your observations below.

1. What nonverbal communication did you observe?

2. What did this communicate to you?

Always communicate encouragement to the people around you. The Bible contains several verses emphasizing the importance of encouragement. I *encourage* you to remember these verses and always encourage the people around you.

- "Therefore encourage one another and build up one another, just as you also are doing" (1 Thessalonians 5:11).
- "Let no unwholesome word proceed from your mouth, but only such a word as is good for edification according to the need of the moment, so that it will give grace to those who hear" (Ephesians 4:29).
- "So then we pursue the things which make for peace and the building up of one another" (Romans 14:19).
- "But encourage one another day after day, as long as it is still called "Today," so that none of you will be hardened by the deceitfulness of sin" (Hebrews 3:13).

In the book of Acts, Paul discusses Barnabas' encouragement of a church: "²³Then when he arrived and witnessed the grace of God, he rejoiced and began to encourage them all with resolute heart to remain true to the Lord; ²⁴for he was a good man, and full of the Holy Spirit and of faith. And considerable numbers were brought to the Lord" (Acts 11:23-24).

What was the outcome of Barnabas' encouragement? Paul said that, "Considerable numbers were brought to the Lord." That's a great outcome for a church. **As you encourage others, they often achieve more. Encouragement is empowerment.**

The impact of encouragement was driven home to me when I spoke with a student who had flunked one of my classes. When she took the course again, I ran into her in the hallway after the first day of class. When she saw me, she immediately looked away and appeared embarrassed. All that changed when I said, "Ya know, I had to repeat a class when I was a college student." She looked directly at me, and I could see the surprise on her face. Her entire demeanor changed. She smiled and said, "Thank you, Dr. Green." She went on to get a PhD. **Make a point to encourage others.**

Communicate appreciation as well as encouragement to the people around you. The apostle Paul tells us: "In everything give thanks; for this is God's will for you in Christ Jesus" (1 Thessalonians 5:18), and, "Always giving thanks for all things in the name of our Lord Jesus Christ to God, even the Father" (Ephesians 5:20).

Appreciation is a powerful force influencing the attitude and motivation of people. When I was in graduate school, I got up at four o'clock one morning to help a fellow graduate student with his research. We drove three hours to the research site, immediately got rained out, and drove three hours back. Another graduate student and I later discussed the fact that we felt taken for granted and that our effort to get up very early and travel six hours was not acknowledged or appreciated. We had no intention to help the following weekend. However, our boss had other ideas, and we indeed went back to help. This time, things turned out differently. We got the work done. But more importantly, when we finished, the graduate student in charge of the research said very sincerely, "Guys, what can I say? Thank you. I could not have done this without your help." I have never forgotten how much my attitude improved when we were shown sincere appreciation. **Always say "thank you" and show sincere appreciation to people who help you and contribute to your success. Be sure to thank God for who He is and for what He does for you!**

Be Clear and Ask for What You Want

Clarity is essential for effective communication. You may assume that the people you talk with can read your mind or just "know" what you are saying. Then you may get frustrated when they don't pick up on your subtle nuances or implications. For example, it is common for a student to talk to me about a problem with a friend or roommate. When I ask if he has talked to the other person, the answer often is "no." He appears to implicitly assume that the other person can and should read his mind and/or simply know what the issues are. This assumption is unrealistic, unfair to the other person, and is quite frustrating to everyone. Furthermore, there is disappointment that the other person doesn't care enough to know what is, or is not, said. This all-to-common situation can be improved simply by talking about the issues with the other person. To avoid this communication problem, **express yourself clearly**. Similarly, **if you don't understand something, ask for clarity**.

Always communicate your expectations clearly. Conflict and stress can often be minimized, if not avoided, by clearly communicating expectations. Unmet expectations cause a lot of conflict, often because the expectations were not understood and/or were unrealistic. Effective communication from the beginning can minimize this source of conflict.

I once asked one of my graduate students for some data I needed to finish an important report. A few days went by, and I had not gotten the data. I was up against a deadline and was annoyed that I hadn't received the data, so I headed to her office to give her a piece of my mind. As I walked to her office and practiced my fire-and-brimstone speech, I had a thought that literally stopped me in my tracks. I was mad because she had missed an important deadline, but I realized I had never given her the deadline. I only said I needed the data. I assumed she would get the data to me by the time I needed it; in other words, I assumed she could read my mind and know the deadline.

From my perspective, she was ignoring my request. In reality, I made a mistake by not giving her a deadline. **When working with others, always clearly define what needs to be done, who will do it, and by when it will be done**; this is sometimes referred as "X (what) by Y (who) by Z (when)." In this example, I should have said I needed the data by a specific date. **Similarly, if you are given a task to accomplish, be sure you know the deadline; if you don't know, ask.**

Failing to define "X by Y by Z" is a common reason that many teams fail to accomplish much. Perhaps you have been on a team in which there is a discussion of what needs to be done, but the work rarely gets done in a timely fashion. For example, if you are planning a cookout for your team, you will decide where to go and how much food to get. Someone will reserve a location and someone will buy the food. These tasks should be assigned to a specific person, and that person needs to know the deadline for completing the task. I have seen this simple process drag on for several weeks because no one takes responsibility for actually doing the work. Or, if the work does get assigned, there is no follow up to ensure it gets done. If you utilize "X by Y by Z," you can avoid these issues.

Akin to clearly communicating your expectations, clearly **ask for what you want.** Have you ever wanted something and were disappointed that you did not get it? If so, did you ask for it? Of course, you won't always get what you want (nor should you), but I think **you will be pleased by the number of times you get what you want simply by asking**. The Bible contains several verses emphasizing the importance of asking God for what you want. God will give you the things that you need and that are best for you.

- "⁷Ask, and it will be given to you; seek, and you will find; knock, and it will be opened to you. ⁸For everyone who asks receives, and he who seeks finds, and to him who knocks it will be opened" (Matthew 7:7–8).

- "If you then, being evil, know how to give good gifts to your children, how much more will your Father who is in heaven give what is good to those who ask Him" (Matthew 7:11).
- "Until now you have asked for nothing in My name; ask and you will receive, so that your joy may be made full" (John 16:24).
- "If you ask Me anything in My name, I will do it." (John 14:14).

God is your loving Father and wants to give you everything He has for you. Remember these verses, and boldly ask God for help when you are in need. The God who raised Jesus from the dead, who held back the Jordan River for the Levitical priests, who parted the Red Sea for Moses, the very God who spoke the world into existence tells you that He will answer you and give you what you ask for. King David says: "Delight yourself in the Lord; And He will give you the desires of your heart" (Psalm 37:4).

Another example of asking for what you want comes from my days in Little League baseball. I wanted to pitch, but my coach never gave me a chance. I complained to my Mom about it, and she asked: "Have you told your coach that you want to pitch?" I answered, "No." Up to that point, I just felt sorry for myself and was developing a grudge against the coach for not letting me pitch. I decided to try Mom's advice. The rest is history—an incredibly average career as a Little League pitcher.

My point is that I asked for what I wanted, and I got it. But more importantly, I learned that I wrongly resented the coach for not letting me pitch; I thought he should "just know" that I wanted to pitch. Thus, I assumed that he thought I could not pitch.

The principle illustrated by this simple childhood example often plays out with adults as well, and this type of incorrect assumption can damage relationships. Perhaps you wanted to "play a position," hold an office in an organization, or be on a team, but you never asked. You may have then been disappointed or even resented that no one asked you. Can you think of examples in which you wanted something, but you did not ask?

In the space below, list three things you want but for which you have not asked. Make a commitment to ask for them.

1.

2.

3.

At this point, it may seem that all you have to do is ask God, and He will give you everything you want. God does not work that way; you must obey Him. Remember that God's salvation is unconditional, but His blessings are not. **If you deliberately disobey God, don't expect His blessings.**

The prophet Samuel made this point to King Saul who disobeyed God: "Has the Lord as much delight in burnt offerings and sacrifices as in obeying the voice of the Lord? Behold, to obey is better than sacrifice, and to heed than the fat of lambs" (1 Samuel 15:22). We see the same principle in the Proverbs: "To do righteousness and justice is desired by the LORD more than sacrifice." (Proverbs 21:3).

The concept of asking for what you want also applies to teamwork. I have found that **many people are happy to help if they are asked.** As a leader, be sure to engage the people around you. By asking for input and for assistance, you will be more effective, and you will find that people will impress you with their abilities. Asking for what you want as a leader has two positive outcomes: First, you are more likely to get what you want. Second, you get your team members involved in your activities.

An Example of Poor Verbal Communication

As I was finishing graduate school and applying for jobs, I attended a professional scientific meeting. In addition to presenting my research, I planned to interview for jobs at the meeting. I passed around my resume to prospective employers and was fortunate to obtain an interview. At the beginning of my interview, a person walked in, introduced himself, and asked for my resume. He took a look at it and said, "Hmm. Well, the topic you've studied for five years is not an area we're interested in." He went on to say, "We're looking for a senior scientist, and you're just finishing your graduate program." So he set my resume down, took off his glasses, clasped his hands in front of him on the desk, leaned back, and asked me, "Why are you here?"

I said, "Sir, thank you for asking that question. Please let me explain." Well, that is what I should have said. Instead, I went nonlinear, and I unloaded on the person. I pointed out that I was invited for the interview and did not appreciate being asked why I came. We were having a heated discussion when a second interviewer came in and explained that the reason I was invited is that I had a PhD in soil science, and the policy of that organization was to interview everybody with a PhD in soil science. Given this information, the original interviewer and I finally calmed down.

I like to use this story to illustrate poor communication and lack of professionalism. First, I was unprofessional in my communication. I raised my voice. I was clearly irritated, and I pointed out their mistakes. In retrospect, although I could not control their actions, I should have controlled my own reaction. I was unprofessional, but I rationalized it because I felt like a "victim." The only thing I could have controlled was my own communication, but I did not.

You should always be professional when communicating. As discussed earlier, nobody can make you mad; only you can make yourself mad. I chose to get mad, and nothing good came out of it. The moral of the story is that **you should take personal responsibility for your communication, regardless of the circumstance.** More broadly, develop the ability to self-regulate (control your emotions in this case) so that you do not respond with your first impulse.

The Bible contains several verses emphasizing the importance of self-control, such as the following:

- "He who is slow to anger has great understanding, But he who is quick-tempered exalts folly" (Proverbs 14:29).
- "A hot-tempered man stirs up strife, But the slow to anger calms a dispute" (Proverbs 15:18).
- "He who guards his mouth and his tongue, Guards his soul from troubles" (Proverbs 21:23).
- "A fool always loses his temper, But a wise man holds it back" (Proverbs 29:11).
- "Do you see a man who is hasty in his words? There is more hope for a fool than for him" (Proverbs 29:20).
- "This you know, my beloved brethren. But everyone must be quick to hear, slow to speak and slow to anger" (James 1:19).

Christians are called to live a life that is worthy of Jesus Christ. To live this type of life, control your emotions and actions. Even if you get angry, control your actions. God provides strength to control yourself through the Holy Spirit: "22But the fruit of the Spirit is love, joy, peace, patience, kindness, goodness, faithfulness, 23gentleness, self-control; against such things there is no law" (Galatians 5:22-23).

Difficult Conversations and Conflict Management

Let's shift gears in our communication discussion to talk about difficult conversations and conflict management, a topic that frequently comes up in my discussions with student leaders. Young Christian leaders must learn to manage conflict because conflict generally gets worse if not managed appropriately.

Difficult conversations and conflict can focus on performance or productivity. As mentioned elsewhere in this book, conflict often arises because of faulty or poorly communicated expectations. Difficult conversations and conflict also can focus on behaviors or convey bad news. Sometimes difficult conversations involve mediation between different groups. You may be the middle person helping to bring people or groups together.

Remember the words of the apostle Paul when you find yourself in a difficult conversation or conflict: "So, as those who have been chosen of God, holy and beloved, put on a heart of compassion, kindness, humility, gentleness and patience" (Colossians 3:12). Showing kindness and compassion or being patient is not necessarily my first reaction when I am in a conflict. You can, though, "put on a heart of compassion" if you ask God to help you handle the conflict.

Furthermore, the apostle Paul tells us: "Be angry, and yet do not sin; do not let the sun go down on your anger" (Ephesians 4:26). Conflict can lead to anger, and controlling your anger can be tough. You can control your emotions when you rely on God's strength rather than your own.

Following are additional verses to understand when facing a conflict:

- "Leave your offering there before the altar and go; first be reconciled to your brother, and then come and present your offering" (Matthew 5:24).

- "If possible, so far as it depends on you, be at peace with all men" (Romans 12:18).
- "So then we pursue the things which make for peace and the building up of one another" (Romans 14:19).
- "Pursue peace with all men, and the sanctification without which no one will see the Lord" (Hebrews 12:14).

These verses show that God wants us to strive for peace. Striving for peace often is contrary to the world's message, but remember Paul's advice to Christians: "And do not be conformed to this world, but be transformed by the renewing of your mind, so that you may prove what the will of God is, that which is good and acceptable and perfect" (Romans 12:2). **In difficult conversations, you must understand the real source of conflict.** Be sure that you **communicate your perspective very clearly, and be sure that you understand the conflict from the perspective of the other person.** In other words, understand the specific problem. Each person should be able to tell his or her side of the story. And each person must have an idea of how he or she wants the conflict to be resolved. **You must provide possible solutions.** Otherwise, you are just complaining, and it is doubtful that you will see improvement.

On numerous occasions, students have come to my office to vent some frustration about a class. I usually let them vent for a while and then ask, "What is the specific problem you want to discuss?" I also ask, "From your perspective, how can this be fixed?" Finally, I ask, "What is your request?" If a student cannot answer these questions, I ask him to think more about it and come back when he can answer my questions.

The point is that you should know the source of conflict and how you want it resolved. For example, if a student tells me that he does not like a class, I can't do much about that. However, if the student says that the teacher always keeps the class five minutes too long, which causes him to be late for his next class, something specific can be addressed.

Additionally, listen actively and completely during difficult conversations because listening indicates you care. Acknowledging the concerns and perspective of the other person is important. Often, you may only want to look at conflict from your perspective; otherwise, **you have to consider that you might be part of the conflict.** This principle is illustrated in Proverbs 18:17: "The first to plead his case seems right, until another comes and examines him."

Look for common ground, such as similar goals or facts you both agree are correct. It's not uncommon to be involved in a difficult conversation and realize that you and the other person are really not that far apart on the issue. If you start by finding that common ground and move forward from there, difficult conversations will be easier.

Several years ago, I was on a committee that was to determine the advising model used by a university. Two different advising models emerged after several hours of heated discussion. Arguing continued with each side pointing out problems with the other model. Finally, a wise person suggested that we focus on the real issue of effective advising. At this point, the conversation focused on the common ground of effective advising. Each side then began to see potential benefits of the other model. We finally agreed that each model would be acceptable and that each college within the university should choose the model that best fit its students and advisers. As long as we focused on our differences, we argued. Once we focused on the common ground, we developed an excellent approach to advising.

As the advising example shows, **the solution to your conflict may be a fair compromise.** To resolve conflict, be flexible and willing to compromise. **Being flexible does not mean that you sacrifice your values or integrity, but it does**

mean that you may not always get exactly what you want. When you're involved in a difficult conversation, focus on the current conflict. Don't drag in old biases and hurts; inclusion of past negativity often makes things worse. Know yourself and your biases. Perhaps the conflict is rooted in your dislike of the person rather than the issue. This reality can be hard to recognize and harder to admit. Is your motive to improve the situation, or is it to attack someone who "has it coming?" For example, consider a conflict between the president and vice president of a student organization. Perhaps the VP is jealous because he was not elected as president. If so, the VP may constantly argue with the president regarding her ideas, not because the ideas are bad but because the VP is upset that he did not get elected as president.

Finally, **there needs to be accountability subsequent to a difficult conversation.** Each person must follow through on the decision that was reached. If not, the person needs to be reminded that he is not doing what he said he would do.

Of course, issues addressed in difficult conversations are not always resolved. However, you must **reach an agreeable outcome, even if you simply agree to disagree.** This outcome provides needed closure and should diminish the likelihood of the situation getting worse. For example, you and your roommate may not reach an agreement on what music you listen to while you study in your dorm room. Rather than continually arguing about it, you simply agree that you don't like the same kind of music. The music that you listen to may not change, but at least you can move on and stop arguing about it.

Now that we have talked about things you should do in a difficult conversation, what are some things you should NOT do during a difficult conversation? (Remember to ask God to help you "put on a heart of compassion...")

1. Don't become accusatory. I've heard it said that whenever you start a statement with "you" (such as "You always..." or "You said..."), the conversation will deteriorate.

2. Don't make things personal. **Try to separate the issue from the person.** For example, if your college roommate leaves his clothes all over your dorm room, talk about the fact that the room is messy (the issue) as opposed to calling your roommate a lazy bum. If you have trouble with that, evaluate your motives.

3. Don't take things personally. This is tough because when somebody is arguing with you, he may try to make it personal.

4. Don't become defensive. Defensiveness is a common reaction during difficult conversations. It's something to guard against, particularly if you know that somebody can easily trip your trigger.

5. Don't immediately dismiss the perspective of the other person. **The person you're having the conflict with may be right.** Just because someone disagrees with you doesn't mean she's not right.

6. Finally, do not immediately give in. If you have prayed and strongly believe in your perspective, stand up for it. **You don't have to give in just because somebody challenges you.** Be sure your motives are pure, your facts are straight, and your assumptions are correct. Be strong and courageous!

Difficult conversations and conflict are going to come your way; if you keep these concepts in mind, you can navigate through to an acceptable outcome.

Here is one more thought to consider: When you find yourself in a conflict and are trying to win, be sure you understand what it means to win. **If you win an argument with a friend but damage or destroy your relationship, you have lost something far more important.** The apostle Paul tells us that, "All things are lawful, but not all things are profitable. All things are lawful, but not all things edify" (1 Corinthians 10:23). If you apply this Biblical principle to the argument with your friend, you realize that just because you *can* win does not mean that you *should* win.

I want to end this section on difficult conversations and conflict with another word of advice: **Get your facts straight before you criticize someone.** When we moved into our first house, we had trouble with the garage door opener. I called the company that made the opener and requested a service call. I mentally rehearsed my chastising speech as I waited for the service person to arrive. When he got to my house, I let him know how dissatisfied I was with his product and company. He showed impeccable professionalism while he listened. He never once interrupted or argued. He simply let me vent. Then, rather than being defensive, he explained the situation to me. His company received several calls like mine. The bottom line was that our contractor had purchased a system that was designed for a single-car garage and installed it in our two-car garage in an effort to save a few bucks. Unfortunately, the smaller motor struggled to raise a larger door, which created a lot of headaches for the garage door company. I apologized for blasting him. And I learned a valuable lesson: **If you are going to criticize someone, be sure you have your facts straight.** This Biblical principle is shown in John 7:51, "Our Law does not judge a man unless it first hears from him and knows what he is doing, does it?" Had I understood this principle, I could have avoided an embarrassing tirade.

Key points from Chapter 5:

1. Be humble and focus on others.

2. Communicate encouragement and appreciation.

3. Be a great listener.

4. Be clear in your content, intent, and context.

5. Communicate your expectations.

6. God wants you to ask Him for what you want.

7. God blesses obedience.

8. Always be professional in your communication.

9. God calls Christians to seek peace rather than conflict.

10. Learn how to manage conflict and have a difficult conversation.

11. Be flexible and willing to make an ethical compromise.

12. If you are going to criticize someone, be sure you have your facts straight.

Please reflect on what you learned in this chapter and answer the following questions:

1. In your own words, explain what it means to communicate effectively.

2. Why is it important to be communicate effectively?

3. What are the three most significant points you learned from this chapter?

4. List three specific things you will work on to be an effective communicator.

5. What benefit will you experience by following through on the items listed in Question 4?

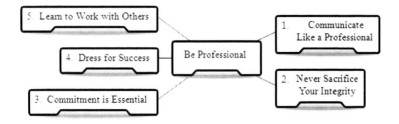

Chapter 6: Be Professional

People often get their impression of Jesus Christ by watching Christians. Thus, Christians must live a life that glorifies Christ. The verses below illustrate the importance of living a life worthy of Christ:

- "Therefore, we are ambassadors for Christ, as though God were making an appeal through us; we beg you on behalf of Christ, be reconciled to God" (2 Corinthians 5:20).
- "In all things show yourself to be an example of good deeds, with purity in doctrine, dignified, sound in speech which is beyond reproach, so that the opponent will be put to shame, having nothing bad to say about us" (Titus 2:7-8).
- "Keep your behavior excellent among the Gentiles, so that in the thing in which they slander you as evil-doers, they may because of your good deeds, as they observe them, glorify God in the day of visitation" (1 Peter 2:12).
- "Only conduct yourselves in a manner worthy of the gospel of Christ, so that whether I come and see you or remain absent, I will hear of you that you are standing firm in one spirit, with one mind striving together for the faith of the gospel" (Philippians 1:27).

In the context of leadership and soft skills, Christians glorify Christ by demonstrating professionalism, which is adherence to standards of behavior in the workplace. The ability to do your job is critical; make no mistake about that. However, **competence is not enough. Other aspects of professionalism are required for success.** Many young people are not fully aware of the expectations of professionalism.

Following are a few components of professionalism:

1. Competence

2. Professional communication

3. Integrity

4. Commitment

5. Appropriate appearance

6. Appreciation for diversity

Communicate Like a Professional

We have already discussed competence, so let's start with professional communication. **Informal communications in the wrong place or at the wrong time suggest lack of professional maturity or respect.** An example for college students is addressing your professor by her first name as opposed to addressing her as "Dr." or "Professor." This distinction is quite important to some faculty. Similarly, I have seen people embarrass themselves by taking too cavalier of an approach to communication with people in authority. This behavior, frankly, is often based on arrogance and can be avoided by heeding the words of the apostle Paul, "Do nothing from selfishness or empty conceit, but with humility of mind regard one another as more important than yourselves" (Philippians 2:3). Another example of unprofessional communication is e-mail that resembles a text message. Avoid "LOL" and similar acronyms. Additionally, use complete sentences when communicating professionally. Although acronyms and short phrases may be acceptable when texting your friends, they are not appropriate for professional communication.

Furthermore, use a dedicated e-mail account for professional correspondence such as applying for college, scholarships, and jobs. Set up an account specifically for your professional correspondence if necessary. I have seen e-mail addresses such as Littleprincess@... or Bullrider@... Unless you are a four-year-old girl in a preschool play or are on the rodeo circuit, these e-mail addresses are inappropriate in a professional setting. Instead, use an e-mail address such as firstname.lastname@... Follow the same principle for the voice mail greeting on your phone. I have called students regarding admission into a university or receipt of a scholarship only to be met with very unprofessional greeting on voice mail. These blunders show professional immaturity and should be avoided.

To be an effective communicator, **create error-free documents**. Your written work represents you and often gives a first impression to a person you may never meet. **An easy way to eliminate errors is to get someone to read a draft of your document**. The person likely will find errors and point out areas that are not clear. I release a document only after it has been reviewed by someone. This simple step can reduce greatly the number of errors in your writing. Keep in mind that if your writing is filled with errors, you send one of four messages: 1) You don't know how to write effectively. 2) You don't care about your work. 3) You don't pay attention to details. 4) You are lazy. None of these messages is flattering.

My experience is that many young people do not worry too much about an error or two in their writing. However, I have seen countless young people be denied awards, scholarships, and even jobs due to errors in written documents. At first approximation, disqualifying a person because of a few errors in an application may seem harsh. However, in a highly competitive process, such as getting a job or a scholarship, small details can make a big difference. **Don't diminish your likelihood of success by submitting application materials that are full of errors.**

Never Sacrifice Your Integrity

Integrity is characterized by high moral and ethical standards and is a hallmark of professionalism. Today, many people act as if there are different shades of right and wrong. The simple fact is that a flaw in your integrity will bring you down sooner or later. When you are ethical, people will recognize your integrity and will respect you for it. King Solomon tells us that, "The integrity of the upright will guide them, But the crookedness of the treacherous will destroy them" (Proverbs 11:3).

Do not negotiate with your integrity. Sometimes the litmus test for integrity is, "This is a little thing," or "No one will know." Let me share my gold-standard illustration of integrity in action. One evening when I was in high school, my Dad was working at our kitchen table. He was an engineer for General Motors and was catching up on some office work. I noticed that he was using a cool mechanical pencil, and I asked if I could have it. He said, "No, you can't have this. It belongs to General Motors." I thought that it was just a pencil, and no one would notice it was missing. Plus, it was such a tiny thing in the realm of the huge corporation. Indeed, I could rationalize him giving me the pencil. Of course, my rationalization was not Biblical. James puts it like this: "Therefore, to one who knows the right thing to do and does not do it, to him it is sin" (James 4:17).

My Dad demonstrated to me that **the standard of integrity is simply to do the right thing**. Would GM have missed the pencil? I doubt it. Would they have even known? Likely not. But those questions are irrelevant. The next day, my Dad stopped at an office supply store and bought me a couple of mechanical pencils. That was about thirty-five years ago, and I still share that story with young people.

I also recall the ethics training I had when I was in law enforcement. The instructor said something that resonated with me: When you act unethically, you jeopardize your integrity, reputation, and career, and you threaten the well-being of your family. She went on to say you would not tolerate someone else doing something so potentially devastating to you. Why, then, would you do it to yourself?

Commitment is Essential

As a Christian, Jesus Christ is your highest commitment. Recall that Jesus once was asked about the greatest commandment: "37And He said to him, 'YOU SHALL LOVE THE LORD YOUR GOD WITH ALL YOUR HEART, AND WITH ALL YOUR SOUL, AND WITH ALL YOUR MIND. 38This is the great and foremost commandment'" (Matthew 22:37–38). I quoted these verses in Part I, Relationships. In the context of relationships, of course, the emphasis was on a *relationship* with Jesus. In the context of commitment, the emphasis is on our *devotion* to Jesus. You are called to love Him with "all your heart and with all your soul and with all your mind." The following verses provide further Biblical principles for the importance of commitment in the life of Christians:

- "If a man makes a vow to the Lord, or takes an oath to bind himself with a binding obligation, he shall not violate his word; he shall do according to all that proceeds out of his mouth" (Numbers 30:2).
- "When you make a vow to the Lord your God, you shall not delay to pay it, for it would be sin in you,

and the Lord your God will surely require it of you" (Deuteronomy 23:21).

- "You shall be careful to perform what goes out from your lips, just as you have voluntarily vowed to the LORD your God, what you have promised" (Deuteronomy 23:23).
- "Offer to God a sacrifice of thanksgiving and pay your vows to the Most High" (Psalm 50:14).
- "⁴When you make a vow to God, do not be late in paying it; for He takes no delight in fools. Pay what you vow! ⁵It is better that you should not vow than that you should vow and not pay" (Ecclesiastes 5:4-5)
- "Again, you have heard that the ancients were told, 'YOU SHALL NOT MAKE FALSE VOWS, BUT SHALL FULFILL YOUR VOWS TO THE LORD'" (Matthew 5:33).

We know that God always honors His commitments and keeps His promises. **As Christians, we must honor our commitments to God and to others. Commitment is foundational to trust, and trust is foundational to success.** We will see in Chapter 11 that God blesses those He can trust, and takes away from those He cannot trust.

Professionalism requires that you honor your commitments. I witnessed a great example of commitment when I was on a fishing trip in Tennessee in high school. My friend Andy and I met an elderly man who offered to take us to his favorite fishing spot if we could meet him the next morning. When we arrived the next morning, the man, who suffered from an advanced case of emphysema, was too sick to take us to his spot. Despite his poor condition, he made a special trip to tell us that he couldn't go and to give us directions so that we could go without him. Needless to say, his effort to honor his word left a lasting impression on us. This man knew he would never see us again, so he could have ignored us with no real consequences. But his standard was not that he could have gotten away without following through; his standard was that he had made a commitment and was going to keep his word. That should be your standard as well.

Don't underestimate the importance of honoring your commitments. Here are a few practical examples of commitment: If you say you will be somewhere at a certain time, be there at that time. If you make a commitment to be a part of a club or organization, show up and make a positive contribution. If you take a class, show up for the class, takes notes, work hard, and turn in your assignments on time. If you say you will do something, do it. If your job requires you to be at work on time, be there on time. **If you can't meet your commitments, inform the person who will be affected as soon as you can.**

What can you do to increase your likelihood of honoring your commitments? As mentioned above, it is better not to make a commitment than to make a commitment that you cannot keep. In the Gospel of Luke we read, "[28]For which one of you, when he wants to build a tower, does not first sit down and calculate the cost to see if he has enough to complete it? [29]Otherwise, when he has laid a foundation and is not able to finish, all who observe it begin to ridicule him" (Luke 14:28-29). The Biblical principle is that you should not start something, or commit to something, unless you have determined that you can finish it appropriately. Furthermore, if you don't honor your commitments, you will be ridiculed, and your reputation will suffer.

I once supervised a brilliant student who was capable of excellent work. In fact, the quality of his work often exceeded my expectations. However, he did not honor his commitments to show up on time and meet deadlines. He incorrectly assumed his work was so good that he did not have to be at his desk or meet deadlines.

I told him that he had committed to work for us, and he was not meeting his commitments. He was quite surprised and argued that he did great work. I agreed with him, but I pointed out that he could lose his job because we could not count on him.

Don't miss this point: You must understand your commitments and honor them. Doing so is foundational to building trust. If you continually fail to honor your commitments, you will jeopardize your success. Honoring part of your commitment is not enough. In this example, the student honored part of his commitment because he did excellent work. However, he did not honor his commitment to be on time and meet deadlines. The nature of his work required him to be in our office at specific times to interact with our staff and contribute to teamwork.

List your pending commitments and make a deliberate plan to honor them:

1.

2.

3.

4.

5.

You **manage your reputation** by honoring commitments. You want to have the reputation that people know they can count on you and that you are ethical. King Solomon says that, "A good name is to be more desired than great wealth, Favor is better than silver and gold" (Proverbs 22:1). If you find that you cannot fulfill a commitment, be sure to inform the person who is counting on you. **You may find reasons or excuses for missing deadlines, but you can't justify failure to communicate that you will miss them.**

Let me share an example of the importance of managing your reputation. I mentored a student on this point several years ago. He was smart and had a great personality. He was liked by nearly everyone. However, he constantly failed to keep his commitments. I had scheduled a mentoring meeting with him, and he missed it. I did not hear anything from him for a few days, so I contacted him to reschedule. He had an excuse for missing the meeting and committed to meet with me later that week. However, he missed the rescheduled meeting. I talked to one of my staff and asked if the student had contacted our office regarding our meeting. My staff shook his head and said, "You can't count on him." (The apostle Luke was right, of course, when he said that you will be ridiculed if you don't honor your commitments.)

The student finally showed up a few days later and tried to use his charm and charisma to downplay the fact that he missed two meetings. I explained to him that he failed to honor his commitment and that he could not charm his way out of it. I further explained my staff's comment on his reputation. The student seemed shocked to hear that he had the reputation of failing to honor his commitments. His realization provided a great teaching opportunity. He did not understand how he was perceived by others. I helped him realize that although he was smart and people really liked him, he must honor his commitments rather than try to schmooze his way out of the consequences. His commitment and reputation improved following our conversation.

Dress for Success

Professionalism requires that you wear appropriate clothing. Remember that you are an ambassador for Christ, and your appearance matters. Your attire should not be a distraction, either positive or negative. I have been involved in several interviews for scholarships, graduate assistantships, jobs, and internships, and I have been amazed by the variety of attire worn by the applicants. Some folks are professionally dressed, and others wear old sweat pants and flip-flops. Nothing shows lack of professionalism and conveys an I-don't-care attitude more than inappropriate attire. Understand that people often associate your appearance with your ability and attitude. Your clothes should be neat and clean and appropriate for your situation.

Never underestimate the importance of being professionally dressed. If you are not sure what attire is appropriate, ask someone. If you still are not sure, it's better to be overdressed than underdressed. I once represented my department and gave a presentation at a university-wide event. I showed up pretty casually dressed. To my surprise (and embarrassment), everyone else who spoke wore a coat and tie. I felt very unprofessional due to way I was dressed. To this day, it's not uncommon for me to be one of the few people at an event wearing a coat and tie because I don't want to make that mistake again.

As a young professional, you likely will encounter two main types of professional dress: business professional and business casual. Business professional attire means that men should wear a conservative, dark-colored suit (matching suit jacket and pants), a shirt with a collar, and a tie. A black belt and matching shoes are also needed. Women should wear a dress, suit, or skirt (the accepted norm is that your skirt be long enough to reach just above your knee) and dress shoes. Business casual, on the other hand, calls for men to wear dress slacks, polos, or sweaters. Women can wear slacks, skirts, blouses, and sweaters. Keep in mind that these guidelines are general. Be sure to check on the accepted clothing norms for your situation.

In a professional setting, avoid wearing jeans, baseball hats, flip-flops, or sweatshirts. Be sure your clothes are clean, fit well, and are free of wrinkles. And be sure to keep your shirt tucked in.

Learn to Work with Others

Professionalism requires that you develop an appreciation for diversity. The Bible provides several verses to guide your thinking when working with others who are different from you:

- "Opening his mouth, Peter said: 'I most certainly understand now that God is not one to show partiality, but in every nation the man who fears Him and does what is right is welcome to Him'" (Acts 10:34-35).
- "For there is no partiality with God" (Romans 2:11).
- "For you are all sons of God through faith in Christ Jesus" (Galatians 3:26).
- "There is neither Jew nor Greek, there is neither slave nor free, there is no male and female, for you are all one in Christ Jesus" (Galatians 3:28).

God does not worry about nationality or background. His unconditional love and grace are available to all people who will accept Him. As Christians, we are to follow His example.

Professionalism requires that you are able to work with people from different cultures and backgrounds. I have always tried to treat others with respect, and I thought that was all I needed to know about working with diverse people. However, several years ago, I attended a diversity workshop where I learned that being nice is important, but is not enough.

Try to understand basic characteristics of fellow students or coworkers who may have different religious, racial, and cultural backgrounds. For example, Americans generally look each other directly in the eye during conversations. In our culture, eye contact suggests that you are interested and are paying attention. In other cultures, direct eye contact may be considered rude. In this case, lack of eye contact would not necessarily indicate that the person is not listening to you; the lack of eye contact simply reflects that person's cultural norm.

People from other cultures may have a different perspective on personal space as well. I have a good friend who is from another country. When he talks, he stands very close to the person he talks to. Doing so is common in his culture. In America, we generally don't stand that close when talking. When we first met, I kept backing up as we talked, and of course, he would step closer again. As our friendship developed, we had a good laugh realizing that we walked when we talked.

The above examples provide very simple illustrations of some common cultural differences you might encounter. A full discussion of interacting with people of different cultures is beyond the scope of this book. The take-home message, though, is that although being nice is important, you should take the time to get to know the people with whom you work or attend school and try to understand a little about their culture. Use this understanding to enhance your ability to work with others.

Professionalism requires that you develop an ability to consider opinions different from your own. Working with other people and considering other opinions can be difficult when you always think you are right or when you don't like the person who has the other perspective. Remember that just because you don't like someone does not mean she cannot have good ideas. Just because a person has a perspective different from yours does not mean he is wrong. Just because someone complains all the time does not mean that the complaint may not be correct occasionally. Often, a valid comment or idea is dismissed because of bias against the person making the comment rather than on the merit of the comment itself. Be on guard for this tendency. Not only is dismissing ideas for this reason unprofessional, but you will also miss some really good ideas.

Professionalism requires that you recognize that others may work differently from you. I am a very linear and direct thinker, and I like to plan things out in nauseating detail and start projects very early with a well-defined plan. I have worked with many highly-productive people who approached projects in nearly the opposite fashion. But the key is that they, too, are capable of high-quality work. This point was driven home for me while I was participating in a national leadership development institute. My cohort consisted of leaders from academia, government, and industry. We had taken several different assessments designed to help us better understand our work style. When the results were returned, we lined up according to styles: Early starters to late starters; planners to non-planners; concrete thinkers to abstract thinkers, and so on. I was surprised to see that the group spanned the entire continuum of work style and approach. The point made—and it was made well—was that there are many effective work styles. Thus, recognize that people may not work like you do, and **be able to work with these people despite your differences.** Be flexible and be able to adapt to your team's approach.

Key points from Chapter 6:

1. Christians are called to live a life that glorifies God.

2. Competence alone is not enough.

3. Create error-free documents.

4. Do not negotiate with your integrity.

5. Commitment is absolutely critical for Christians.

6. Manage your reputation.

7. Make a positive statement with your appearance.

8. Consider perspectives that are different from your own.

9. Make an effort to understand basic characteristics of your coworkers and classmates.

Please reflect on what you learned in this chapter and answer the following questions:

1. In your own words, explain what it means to be professional.

2. Why is it important to be professional?

3. What are the three most significant points you learned from this chapter?

4. List three specific things you will work on to be professional.

5. What benefit will you experience by following through on the items listed in Question 4?

Chapter 7: Develop Synergies

Synergy occurs when the sum of the component parts of a system is greater than is the sum of the individual parts. The Bible contains an excellent description of synergy: "⁹Two are better than one because they have a good return for their labor. ¹⁰For if either of them falls, the one will lift up his companion. ¹¹Furthermore, if two lie down together they keep warm, but how can one be warm alone? ¹²And if one can overpower him who is alone, two can resist him. A cord of three strands is not quickly torn apart" (Ecclesiastes 4:9-12).

Let's talk more about a "cord of three strands." You probably know that rope is made by weaving several small, individual strands together. The individual strands are not particularly strong. But when the strands are wound together, a strong rope is formed. As Christians, we must be sure that Jesus Christ is a strand in everything we do. **There is no greater manifestation of synergy, where the system greatly exceeds the sum of the individual parts, than when a Christian allows Jesus Christ to work in and through his or her life.**

Synergy is a key advantage of teamwork. **Synergy occurs as a team of people works together toward a common goal, and the outcome is greater than if the people had worked alone. However, synergy does not occur just because people are on the same team.** For example, perhaps you have seen a basketball team that had great individual players, but the players did not work together, so the team did not perform well.

Similarly, a collection of talented people on the same team in your class or on your job may not actually be working together. If the people are not sharing ideas, giving feedback, and having meaningful discussions, synergy will not occur. My experience is that many "teams" of young people never achieve synergy because team members are not motivated enough to engage in meaningful discussion. These teams struggle and/or never accomplish what they should because team members do not work effectively together, even though each person may be talented. Team meetings are boring, and projects are completed poorly. Thus, many young people think teamwork is a drag, which is unfortunate for two reasons: First, teamwork can be very gratifying if done correctly. Second, the discussions and interactions that underlie true synergy result in a better outcome. Following is an example of how synergy improved this book.

While discussing synergy with a student who read a draft of this manuscript, I realized that I had not explained synergy adequately. As he and I discussed synergy, I developed a better explanation of synergy. I laughed and told him that our conversation was exactly what synergy was about. His questions and feedback resulted in an improved discussion. When people truly work together, the outcome very often exceeds what can be accomplished without working together.

Diversity Revisited

Whether you are in high school, college, or the workforce, you will work in teams from time to time. Realize that **more-diverse teams generally are more productive than less-diverse teams.** You may think about gathering teams of people who are just like you because if they're like you, they must be great people. However, teams should include people who are different from you, including people with unique perspectives, approaches, experiences, cultural backgrounds, insight, and expertise.

It's very important that you **take full advantage of the diversity of your team**. People who are different from you will provide ideas and perspectives that can enrich your team. And, of course, your perspective is valuable as well. To achieve synergy, each person must speak up, be heard, and make her unique contribution. **An effective team engages all members, and an effective leader gets all team members working together toward a common goal.**

The Bible contains an excellent description of the need for and value of different members of team. The apostle Paul tells us:

> [14]For the body is not one member, but many. [15]If the foot says, 'Because I am not a hand, I am not a part of the body,' it is not for this reason any the less a part of the body. [16]And if the ear says, 'Because I am not an eye, I am not a part of the body,' it is not for this reason any the less a part of the body. [17]If the whole body were an eye, where would the hearing be? If the whole were hearing, where would the sense of smell be? [18]But now God has placed the members, each one of them, in the body, just as He desired (1 Corinthians 12:14–18).

These verses illustrate important principles to guide team work. First, just as a body needs different parts, teams need members with different abilities and expertise. Second, although different, each member is important and has an important role to fulfill. Finally, all the members must be moving towards the same goal. Imagine that your feet have the goal to run to the left, but your eyes want to look to the right. What will happen? Sooner or later, you are going to stumble. A team that contains members who are not moving toward the same goal also will encounter difficulty. An effective leader assures that all members of her team are moving towards a common goal.

Although all team members must be engaged, as a young person, recognize the importance of diversity based on experience. When I was in high school, I had a conversation with a neighbor who had worked in industry for several years. He shared a story with me about his work as a senior member of a team; the rest of the team consisted of recent college graduates. The recent graduates were well educated, but they didn't have much experience. Despite their great academic training, they could not solve the problem they were working on. However, my neighbor solved it. He told me that the recent graduates looked at him as if to say, "Wow, how did the old dude figure that out?" He told them he learned something several years before while working on another project, and that experience led him to the solution for the current problem. **Diversity of experience is important, as is diversity of background, expertise, and perspective.** Recognize and appreciate the experience of those who have "been there," especially when starting a new job. This principle is made in the Bible: "Wisdom is with aged men, with long life is understanding" (Job 12:12).

Also keep in mind that some people on your team may be difficult to work with. Professionalism requires the ability to function as a team member. **Put aside biases so that you can work with a wide range of people.** And, of course, be sure you are not the difficult person in the group.

Finally, realize that you must be self-motivated and be able to complete your tasks when working as part of a team. Remember the "I in Team" concept discussed earlier in the book and use your strengths to help your team succeed. Perhaps you have heard the saying, "A chain is only as strong as its weakest link." The same principle applies to teamwork. Always put forth your best effort so that you are not the weakest link on your team.

There is another way to look at this: "Now he who plants and he who waters are one; but each will receive his own reward according to his own labor" (1 Corinthians 3:8). In other words, you will be rewarded based on your contribution. Individuals who make strong contributions to a team eventually will see their own advancement. In my leadership roles, I have promoted or provided resources to individuals who made major contributions to teams.

In my own career, I was active on a recruiting and retention team in my department. I worked hard and made contributions. Soon, I was moved to a team at the college level (one level higher than the department team). I continued to make a difference, and eventually I was selected to lead the college team and also lead an important New Student Orientation program. When a leadership position opened up at the college level, I was promoted and received a significant salary increase. That position led to a position with greater responsibility and greater salary at another university. The point is that if you work hard and contribute to your team, sooner or later, you will be rewarded as an individual. (Remember that God has established your steps!)

In the space below, discuss your best and your worst experiences working on a team or collaborating with others.

1. What worked well in your best experience?

2. What problems did you encounter in the worst experience?

3. How were the problems addressed?

Keep Responsibility Where it Belongs

Keep responsibility where it belongs when working with others. We read in Galatians 6:5 that: "For each one will bear his own load." In other words, do not let someone give his problems to you to solve. Doing someone else's work is a common temptation for leaders. It is natural to want to help those people with whom you work. The repercussions, however, are important: First, if you spend your time doing someone else's work, you may not have enough time to do your own work; focusing on your work is important for completing your priorities. Second, you demonstrate to the person who gives you his work that he can bring you work and you will do it, which sets a bad precedent. Third, the person does not have to learn how to complete the task himself, which denies him an opportunity to grow.

As just discussed, you don't want to "own" the work of others. However, **ownership in your work can be a great motivator**. Consider this example: I was a co-author on a paper that was to be presented by a graduate student at a national meeting. She was unable to attend the meeting due to the pending birth of a child. The student prepared the presentation and gave it to me. I appreciated her effort, but I could not get excited about the presentation in its current form. So I began to make a few changes. Before long, the presentation was quite different. There were no substantive changes in content (she had done an excellent job preparing the presentation), but I tweaked it enough to make it mine. Was it a better presentation? No, not at all. But now I "owned" it. I was surprised how much my attitude about giving the presentation improved. I learned the importance of buying into something to make it my own. Once the presentation became something I invested time in, it took on a new value.

As you work with others, remember that many people care about their work, and caring is a powerful motivator. Leaders can diminish this motivation by giving too much input into a person's work. **When telling someone how you think her work can be improved, be sure not to squash her creativity and enthusiasm**.

Early in my career as a leader, I gave input to two of my staff who were making a student recruitment brochure. I told them very specifically what words to delete, what words to add, what new picture was needed, and so on. As I gave my input, I noticed that the staff were quickly losing their enthusiasm for a project that they had originally enjoyed working on. I learned the hard way the lesson that I am conveying here. On subsequent projects, rather than telling them exactly what to do and destroying their enthusiasm, I would make comments such as, "What do you think about making the brochure show more interaction between faculty and students?" This approach worked well. Instead of telling them exactly what to do, I gave them a vision for what I wanted, and then let them figure out the best way to do it. The final brochure looked great, and it showed what I wanted to show. My staff did a great job because they "owned" it and were motivated to make an excellent brochure.

Don't make a habit of giving your problems to your boss. This activity sends the message that you cannot do your work. When necessary, seek help from your boss, but don't drop off work in her office. **If you take a question to your boss, take some potential answers**. If one of my staff brings a problem to me, the first question I ask is, "What do you recommend?" If she does not have an answer, I ask her to keep thinking about it and come back when she has a couple of ideas.

Let's end this section with a discussion on delegation, which refers to the process of a leader giving tasks to the people who work for her. The Bible contains an excellent example of the importance of delegation. In the book of Exodus, we read that Moses is serving as a judge for the people of Israel and receives helpful advice from his father-in-law.

> [17]Moses' father-in-law said to him, "The thing that you are doing is not good. [18]You will surely wear out, both yourself and these people who are with you, for the task is too heavy for you; you cannot do it alone. [19]Now listen to me: I will give you counsel, and God be with you. You be the people's representative before God, and you bring the disputes to God, [20]then teach them the statutes and the laws, and make known to them the way in which they are to walk and

the work they are to do. [21]Furthermore, you shall select out of all the people able men who fear God, men of truth, those who hate dishonest gain; and you shall place these over them as leaders of thousands, of hundreds, of fifties and of tens. [22]Let them judge the people at all times; and let it be that every major dispute they will bring to you, but every minor dispute they themselves will judge. So it will be easier for you, and they will bear the burden with you" (Exodus 18:17-22).

Several important principles are illustrated in these verses. First, notice that Moses was mentored by his father in law. We will discuss mentoring in the next chapter. Second, the fact that Moses was doing all the work himself was "not good" for Moses or for the people. Sometimes, even when you work hard, you are not doing what is best for yourself or those around you. When you try to do too much, quality likely will suffer, and details may be missed. Third, Moses was instructed to select and train competent people to help. This point is important; you must train your people, and they must be qualified to handle the work you delegate to them. Finally, Moses made clear what his delegates could do (judge minor disputes) and what he would do (judge major disputes).

When I was in graduate school, I was the supervisor for the hourly workers in our research group. One day I was assigning tasks to one of our laboratory workers. He listened patiently to my list, and then he said, "If I were the boss, I would do this myself." Without thinking, I responded, "That is why you are not the boss." At the time, I was merely trying to be funny. However, that statement is very true. To be successful as a leader, you must delegate. **An effective leader delegates tasks that others can do, so that the leader can focus effort on tasks that only he can do.** Of course, a leader should lend a hand occasionally to show that he is not "too good" to help his team; this effort helps maintain a good rapport. For example, I would occasionally empty our office recycling bin, reload paper into the copy machine, and help unload soil samples when my crew returned from research sites.

In addition to delegating the work, leaders must delegate the authority to complete the work. Articulate your desired outcomes and deadlines (X by Y by Z), and then get out of the way. Don't micromanage to the point that you kill the enthusiasm and creativity of the talented people who work with you. Finally, be sure to follow up as needed to hold the person accountable and ensure that work is getting done.

Key points from Chapter 7:

1. You can accomplish more in a team environment than when working alone.

2. You can accomplish more with God than you can without Him.

3. Embrace diversity on your team.

4. Work hard and contribute to your team.

5. Don't squash the creativity and enthusiasm of others.

6. Keep responsibility where it belongs.

7. If you take a problem to your boss, always take a solution.

8. Delegate tasks that someone else can do for you so that you can focus your efforts on the tasks that only you can do.

Please reflect on what you learned in this chapter and answer the following questions:

1. In your own words, explain what it means to develop synergies.

2. Why is it important to develop synergies?

3. What are the three most significant points you learned from this chapter?

4. List three specific things you will work on to develop synergies.

5. What benefit will you experience by following through on the items listed in Question 4?

Chapter 8: Embrace Mentoring

This book includes numerous examples of advice, input, and perspective I received from people who were wiser and more experienced than I. When you embrace mentoring, you make more rapid progress in developing your leadership and soft skills. When you help others on their journey, you too can make a positive impact on their lives. **Mentoring, the process of helping others develop, is a powerful catalyst for improvement.** Furthermore, a mentor can be a great networking contact for you.

The Bible has several verses describing the importance of mentoring, including the following:

- "Where there is no guidance the people fall, But in abundance of counselors there is victory" (Proverbs 11:14).
- "The way of a fool is right in his own eyes, But a wise man is he who listens to counsel" (Proverbs 12:15).
- "Through insolence comes nothing but strife, But wisdom is with those who receive counsel" (Proverbs 13:10).
- "Without consultation, plans are frustrated, But with many counselors they succeed" (Proverbs 15:22).
- "Incline your ear and hear the words of the wise, And apply your mind to my knowledge" (Proverbs 22:17).

- "For by wise guidance you will wage war, And in abundance of counselors there is victory" (Proverbs 24:6).
- "The things which you have heard from me in the presence of many witnesses, entrust these to faithful men who will be able to teach others also" (2 Timothy 2:2).

As you can see, God puts a premium on receiving guidance from wise people. **A Christian should always seek God's guidance.** As discussed elsewhere, you can be confident that God will answer you, give you wisdom, and show you the correct path to choose. God tells us in the Psalms: "I will instruct you and teach you in the way which you should go; I will counsel you with My eye upon you" (Psalm 32:8). Be sure to read your Bible every day because it is an excellent source of God's mentoring. The apostle Paul says that, "16All Scripture is inspired by God and profitable for teaching, for reproof, for correction, for training in righteousness; 17so that the man of God may be adequate, equipped for every good work" (2 Timothy 3:16-17). Of course, God also can speak to you through a Christian mentor.

Get Yourself a Mentor

Years ago, while in Sunday School, we were asked to discuss a person who made a significant impact on our lives. Nearly everyone named a person who mentored him or her in high school or college. **This period of your life is the ideal time to find a mentor.**

I have had informal mentoring relationships with colleagues, a formal mentorship with an executive coach, and a peer mentorship with a trusted colleague. **Most successful people have a mentor they turn to for advice.** Several examples of mentoring are found in the Bible: Jesus mentored His disciples; the prophet Elijah mentored Elisha; Moses mentored Joshua; Paul mentored Timothy. I still have mentors from whom I seek advice.

When I was a freshman in college, I had a class with a senior. He had changed his major and needed to go back and finish an entry-level math class. He was a great mentor for me. He gave lots of practical advice that a freshman needed to hear. I doubt he felt like a mentor, but he gave me great perspective on balancing life and school, taking tests, and college life in general.

In graduate school, I had a remarkable mentor in my major professor, Dr. A.M. Blackmer. He took a naïve kid with an unhealthy balance of arrogance and ignorance and turned that kid into a scientist. The value he added to me has changed my life. People often say that circumstances, events, or people "changed my life," but Dr. Blackmer truly did. He taught me to be a scientist, and he set me on a path to achieve much more than I ever could have had I not worked with him. **An effective mentor can greatly enhance your leadership and soft-skills development.**

Although mentoring relationships can be formal, they need not be. I had a very impactful conversation with a professor who gave me excellent advice that changed the way I looked at my position as an assistant professor. He and I had a weekly lunch together and talked about what it takes to be a professor. One particular piece of advice he gave me really made a difference. He told me to publish papers on teaching as well as on research when I started my faculty position. At that point in my career, it did not occur to me to publish on teaching. I was naïve. I took his advice and got a couple of publications on teaching. One of these publications was the most-read manuscript in an education journal for two consecutive months. Of all the papers I have published, that one is my favorite. Had I not gotten that advice from him, I likely would not have even thought to publish that paper. Recall an earlier point: **A single experience can put your development on an entirely different trajectory**. This experience came to me through informal mentoring.

In some cases, mentoring is specific. For example, I often mentor students on how to prepare for and take exams, how to manage their time, and how to utilize best-practices for student success. The advice I give is very specific regarding what needs to be done, and the advice is tailored to the individual person.

Another type of mentoring focuses on helping a person see different perspectives when making decisions. In this case, there may not be a single, right answer. For example, if I mentor a student who is selecting a major or trying to decide which internship to take, we often talk about the pros and cons of each choice. Doing so allows the student to make an informed decision after considering various options.

I could share several more examples of great mentors in my life, including my parents. **Take advantage of every opportunity to learn from others who have more experience, different experience, or a different perspective.** My life has been improved greatly by the advice and efforts of others who invested time in me. **I encourage you to find impactful mentors, and also to mentor others.**

Following are some characteristics of an ideal Christian mentor:

1. Genuine, discernable knowledge of God's word

2. Real desire to see you succeed

3. Willingness to invest a reasonable amount of time with you

4. Perspective and experience different from yours

5. Credibility to give valuable advice

6. Courage to be honest

7. Commitment to hold you accountable

8. Compassion to be patient

As a Christian, seek a Christian mentor so that the advice given is consistent with God's word. An effective mentor has a genuine desire to help you succeed. **Seek someone who cares about your success.** A mentor should have a reasonable amount of time to spend with you so that you can have unhurried discussions. Select a mentor who can give perspectives you may not have. **Don't expect your mentor always to tell you what to do; rather, expect her to help you see things from various perspectives.** Seeing things from a variety of perspectives helps you make informed decisions. Your mentor needs the courage to tell you things you may not want to hear, to help you see things you may not see, and he needs to hold you accountable for considering the input. Finally, seek a mentor who will be patient with you as you grapple with your issues and decisions.

If you do not have a mentor, you definitely should find one. As mentioned earlier, you might ask a teacher, coach, community leader, or pastor. You might select a mentor based on your career goal. For example, if you want to work in the banking industry, seek a mentor from the leadership of a bank in your community. Or perhaps you want to focus on a specific trait, such as communication. In this case, seek out a person who is an excellent communicator. Once you have identified a potential mentor, don't be shy about talking to him. Even in today's fast-paced, hectic world, most people are happy to invest time in a young person who is trying to improve his skills.

List three potential mentors. Make a commitment to discuss mentoring with each of them.

1.

2.

3.

As a conversation starter, tell your potential mentor that you are developing your leadership and soft skills and would like her help. Anticipate that your potential mentor will ask what you want to focus on and will likely ask about your goals. Be sure to have given some thought about a few specific areas and goals. For example, you may want to focus on professionalism; if so, share that with your potential mentor. If your mentor works in a career in which you would like to work, ask for advice on the experiences, education, and skills needed to succeed in that career. Ask if you can shadow him for a day or two while he works. Finally, ask about her availability and indicate how much time you would like to spend with her. For example, you may ask if she would could meet for an hour once or twice a month.

Make the Most of Your Mentoring Opportunity

Once you find a mentor, commit fully to the mentoring process. Following is a list of characteristics that are important for you as the mentee:

1. Desire to succeed

2. Accountability

3. Preparedness

4. Willingness to be coached

5. Courage to accept constructive criticism

6. Appreciation

Mentoring only will be as successful as you make it. If you don't have a true commitment to succeed, then the best advice from your mentor won't have a real impact. Commitment requires accountability, which includes thinking deeply about the input you get and following through as appropriate. Accountability also includes punctuality on your part and respect for the schedule of your mentor. Arrive at your meetings on time and be committed to stopping at the appointed time. Be sure that you complete any assignments that your mentor gives you. Don't forget the importance of professional dress; you want to make a good impression. Also, have a list of questions/topics to discuss. Be sure that you have thought through these items and **be prepared** to discuss your ideas.

You must be willing to be coached. In other words, **be willing to consider the input of your mentor.** Your mentor may give specific advice on what you need to do, or she may help you see multiple solutions or options rather than telling you specifically what to do. Thus, be willing to consider different perspectives, which can be challenging. I have worked with some young people who were committed to success, but who were not coachable. Basically, they had their minds made up and did not consider the other perspectives we discussed. **You must be willing to accept constructive criticism that may be difficult to hear.** If you have selected the right mentor, the feedback will be constructive and will help you grow. Finally, show your appreciation and gratitude to your mentor for investing in your success.

Key points from Chapter 8:

1. Find a Christian mentor.

2. Pray to God and let Him mentor you.

3. Be a mentor to others.

4. Don't expect your mentor always to tell you what to do.

5. Be coachable.

6. Be committed.

Please reflect on what you learned in this chapter and answer the following questions:

1. In your own words, explain what it means to embrace mentoring.

2. Why is it important to have a mentor?

3. What are the three most significant points you learned from this chapter?

4. List three specific things you will work on for mentoring.

5. What benefit will you experience by following through on the items listed in Question 4?

Part III: Results

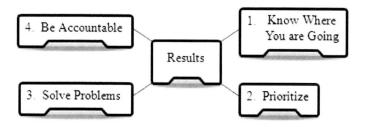

4. Be Accountable

1. Know Where You are Going

Results

3. Solve Problems

2. Prioritize

You must focus on results if you want to be successful. Focusing on effort is quite easy, but the ultimate measure of success is impactful results. Realize that effort (activity) and accomplishment (producing results) are not the same. Similarly, busyness (doing something) is not the same thing as productivity (doing something important). These are powerful concepts to understand and apply to your life.

The apostle Paul tells us: "Do you not know that those who run in a race all run, but only one receives the prize? Run in such a way that you may win" (1 Corinthians 9:24). He admonishes us not just to run, but run to win. This principle should guide Christians in general, but is particularly impactful for young Christians who are developing leadership and soft skills.

Throughout this book, I have shown through Scripture how God has promised to help you, strengthen you, equip you, and give you abundance. Although this is true, Christians can't just sit back, do nothing, and expect God to bring success to them. Note that Paul says, "Run in such a way that you may win." The message is clear. **You have to work hard and do your best. Pray to God and ask Him to empower you.**

If you focus on achieving impactful results, and if you truly "run," then one day you can look back on your life and say what Paul said: "I have fought the good fight, I have finished the course, I have kept the faith" (2 Timothy 4:7). It is gratifying to live your life such that you achieve everything that God has planned for you.

Of course, to be productive, to do something important, you must know what is important. In other words, ask God to work in and through your life and use His plan to shape your values, goals, and priorities. Learn to be future-oriented and invest time in activities today that will benefit your future.

If you want to achieve impactful results, you must solve problems. Defining a problem is an important step. It has been said that once you have defined a problem, you have it half-solved. Furthermore, solving problems will increase your potential for opportunity, rewards, and success.

Finally, be accountable for your attitude, effort, and behavior. Accountability requires that you put forth your best effort. Many young people fail to achieve what they are capable of achieving simply because they do not put forth enough effort. Accountability requires you to admit your mistakes, learn from them, and then move on.

Chapter 9: Know Where You Are Going

Many people drift through life without any real direction or plan. These people may find some measure of success, but they may not. You achieve success by figuring out God's plan for your life and then deliberately moving toward it.

The Target

I have shared several stories with you, but the following story makes one of the most important points I want to make in this book. While living in Texas, I obtained my peace officer license and was a commissioned peace officer. I served with some great individuals and had access to excellent training. I had the opportunity to take in-depth training on handgun shooting. For three days, we practiced several drills and developed a lot of skill. We learned the "science" of shooting, and we also developed practical skills.

We shot several qualification courses during the three days, but we had to shoot one final official qualification to pass the course. I had done very well in earlier qualifications. I was trained, competent, and ready. We lined up and faced our targets twenty-five yards away. As we began our official qualification course, my shots were finding their target. My shooting was not perfect, but I was doing well.

Everything was great until the lieutenant said, "Cary!" I responded, "Yes, sir??" "You are shooting at the wrong target!" "What??!!!" He repeated, "You are shooting at the wrong target!" Well, I had two thoughts, the first of which is not repeatable in a Christian book. But my second thought was this: What an incredible metaphor for life. Despite my bruised pride (cops love opportunities like this to razz a fellow officer), I knew I had a great story to share with young people.

Life is a lot like that experience on the range. I was trained and competent, doing my job, and I was getting an excellent score. But it was all for nothing because I was shooting at the wrong target. And I did not even know it—a key point. **You may be so absorbed in what you are doing that you lose sight of the fact that you may be shooting at the wrong target.** This can be especially difficult to recognize when you are "shooting well."

What, then, is the right target? The right targets for you are goals that align with your God-given values and that lead you to achieve God's plan for your life. Learn from this illustration and **always invest your time and use your skills to work towards something meaningful.** In other words, develop goals that align with what is important to you. Then prioritize your time and laser-focus your effort to achieve those goals. Don't waste time shooting at the wrong target.

As a Christian, your targets are those things that are consistent with God's priorities for your life. Following are a few key verses outlining God's priorities:

- "And He said to him, 'YOU SHALL LOVE THE LORD YOUR GOD WITH ALL YOUR HEART, AND WITH ALL YOUR SOUL, AND WITH ALL YOUR MIND.' 38This is the great and foremost commandment. 39The second is like it, 'YOU SHALL LOVE YOUR NEIGHBOR AS YOURSELF'" (Matthew 22:37-39).

- "He has told you, O man, what is good; And what does the LORD require of you But to do justice, to love kindness, And to walk humbly with your God" (Micah 6:8)?
- "If you love Me, you will keep My commandments." (John 14:15).
- "But seek first His kingdom and His righteousness, and all these things will be added to you" (Matthew 6:33).
- "'For I know the plans that I have for you,' declares the Lord, 'plans for welfare and not for calamity to give you a future and a hope'" (Jeremiah 29:11).
- "19Go therefore and make disciples of all the nations, baptizing them in the name of the Father and the Son and the Holy Spirit, 20teaching them to observe all that I commanded you; and lo, I am with you always, even to the end of the age" (Matthew 28:19-20).

Once again we see that God's top priority is for us to love Him, and to love others as well. We are to be humble, kind, and do justice. One of the ways we show God that we love Him is to obey His commandments. As imperfect humans, we occasionally will stumble in our obedience, but God will forgive us. The point is that if you truly love God, your target is to avoid deliberate and willful sin. If you put a priority on seeking God's will, He will provide what we need. Our targets must include the plans that God has for each of us. Finally, Christians are called to spread the Gospel of Jesus Christ so that others may receive salvation through forgiveness and experience the best of God's blessings.

Make Success Personal

To enjoy the best life that God has for you, make God's values your values, make God's goals your goals, and make God's priorities your priorities. When I refer to "your priorities" and "things that are important to you," I refer to those things that God reveals to you according to His plan for your life.

Before we go too much further, let's define some terms:

- **Values** are those things that truly are important to you. Values should be God-given and guide your overall direction in life. Your values provide foundational context for your goals and priorities. Values are fairly stable over time.
- **Goals** are results or accomplishments you want to achieve. Goals should align with God's plan for your life and with your values.
- **Priorities** are those things that God deems as important to you (based on His plan for your life) and that should preferentially receive your time, effort, and resources. Focusing effort on your priorities will enable you to reach your goals and experience the abundant and successful life God has for you.

For example, if you value volunteerism, your goal may be working at the local homeless shelter. You prioritize your time by working at the shelter rather than doing something else.

Because your values are foundational, first determine your values. To begin, refer to the Life Balance exercise in Chapter 3. Also, please think back to how you described "living a successful life" in the same chapter. Expand those exercises to help you further identify your values by answering a few more questions:

1. What is God's plan for your life?

2. What are you truly passionate about?

3. What are your greatest accomplishments?

4. Think about the times you have been the happiest. What contributed to your happiness?

5. What are you doing when "time flies"?

6. How would you like to be described by family and friends?

Providing an exhaustive list of values is beyond the scope of this book, but the questions above coupled with the earlier exercises will give you insight into your values. I encourage you to seek resources beyond this book as you identify your values. Pray to God and ask Him to reveal His values for you. If you are a student, contact your advisor, counselor, or career center to identify resources available to you. Ask your mentor to help you identify your values. Additionally, you can find information online regarding determining your values.

Don't worry if identifying your values seems overwhelming at first. **Your values are very important, and it may take time to develop a list of your true values.** To provide an example, following is a list of my values:

1. My relationship with Jesus Christ

2. My wife and daughter

3. Leadership

4. Excellence

5. Adding value to others

6. Health and fitness

7. Professional development

8. Production capacity

Based on what you have determined so far, list your values.

1.

2.

3.

4.

5.

Do's and Don'ts for Setting and Achieving Goals

As just discussed, be sure your goals align with God's plan for your life. Pursuing goals outside of God's plan will not bring the abundant and successful life that God has for you. Although you may achieve some success, you will not achieve the very best that God has for you. And you will not experience the joy, peace, and blessing that only come from walking in step with Jesus Christ.

King David wrote this advice to his son, Solomon: "Unless the Lord builds the house, they labor in vain who build it; Unless the Lord guards the city, the watchman keeps awake in vain" (Psalm 127:1). A similar message is given in Proverbs 19:21: "Many plans are in a man's heart, But the counsel of the Lord will stand." The principle illustrated in these verses is that **you will "labor in vain" unless your goals and activities line up with God's plan for your life.** Ask God to reveal His plan as you set goals for your life. He will answer you.

Let's look more deeply at aligning our goals with God's plan. Think back to the "futility treatments" example I shared earlier. My wife and I wanted to have a child, and we pursued fertility treatments. However, God's plan was that we adopt a child. You may wonder why I am convinced *now* that God's plan was for us to adopt a child. I am convinced now because the fertility treatments did not work, but adoption did work.

Had I sought God's plan more genuinely through prayer, we likely would have skipped the fertility treatments and instead began the adoption process. And we likely could have avoided a lot of heartache and expense. Of course, God used our experience "for good" as He promised in Romans 8:28. We now have a child. Furthermore, I learned a valuable lesson that I can share with you. **Seek God's guidance and follow His plan rather than asking Him to bless your plan. Indeed, it is futile to try to do things your way instead of God's way.**

The Bible provides in the book of Jonah another example of what happens when you shoot at your own target rather than following God's plan. God told Jonah to preach in Nineveh. However, Jonah got in a boat and went in a different direction. Jonah eventually was thrown into the sea. A big fish swallowed Jonah and tossed him on the beach three days later. The Bible says that when Jonah got back on dry land: "¹Now the word of the LORD came to Jonah the second time, saying, '²Arise, go to Nineveh the great city and proclaim to it the proclamation which I am going to tell you'" (Jonah 3:1-2). This time Jonah followed God's plan. The result was that the people of Nineveh repented and received God's forgiveness.

God valued the repentance of the people of Nineveh. His ultimate goal was their salvation, and His priority was "proclaiming" to the people of Nineveh. Jonah, however, initially ignored God's values, goals, and priorities. What can we learn from this story? First, Jonah suffered for not immediately following God's plan. Second, Jonah ultimately did what God called Him to do, and God's goal was achieved. **God's goals**

always are achieved. You are wise to seek His values, goals, and priorities for your life.

In the space below, develop a specific goal for your God-given values. For example, I value my relationship with Jesus Christ, leadership, adding value to others, and professional development. For these values, I have the following goal: writing a book on leadership and soft-skills development for young Christians.

Value(s): <u>Relationship with Jesus Christ, Leadership, adding value to others, and professional development.</u>

Goal: <u>Write a book on leadership and soft skills for young Christians.</u>

Value(s):_____
Goal 1:_____

Value(s):_____
Goal 2:_____

Value(s):_____
Goal 3:_____

Now that you have set a few goals, realize that **setting goals is not enough; you must be willing and able to achieve them**. Indeed, many people who set goals never achieve them. Before we talk about achieving our goals, let's discuss why some goals aren't achieved.

My own experiences and my experiences working with young people have convinced me that many goals are not aligned with God's plan. **Goals not aligned with God's plan for your life and not aligned with your God-given values**

never should have been set. Time spent chasing these bogus goals detracts from effort that could be (and should be) spent achieving values-aligned goals.

Furthermore, when challenges come, **you won't demonstrate real commitment to goals that are not anchored firmly to your values.** A classic example is starting an exercise program at the beginning of a new year. If you don't value exercise, this artificial goal quickly loses momentum; it never had a chance. The result is wasted time. And you may beat yourself up for not reaching a goal, even a goal that never should have been set. A much more insidious effect is that you can become desensitized to failing to achieve goals, thereby conditioning yourself to letting your values-aligned goals go unrealized. However, if your goals are aligned with God's plan, He will strengthen you to achieve the goals.

So how do you set and achieve goals? (The first step, of course, is to seek God's guidance.) You should set short-term (days and weeks) goals, medium-term (months) goals, and long-term (years) goals. Think back to my discussion of doing statistics to publish my research to reach my goal of promotion and tenure. My long-term goal was to receive promotion and tenure; it required six years. To reach this long-term goal, I needed to write several publications, a medium-term goal that took a few months. To write the publications, I needed to do several things, one of which was statistics. Thus, I set some short-term goals prioritized on statistically analyzing my research data. As we discussed in "Keep Things in Proper Context," I worked on the statistics (short-term goal) for a few days, which contributed to my publications (medium-term goal), which contributed to my long-term goal of promotion and tenure.

A critical first step in setting goals, regardless of their duration, is to align your goals with what is truly important to you. Take a minute to review the previous discussion on values. Once you know your values, determine what you want to accomplish. These accomplishments are your goals. Following are some steps that will help you achieve your goals:

1. Align your goals with God's plan.

2. Define the outcomes of your goals.

3. Define the benefits of your goals.

4. Identify the major steps required to achieve your goals.

5. Stay focused on priorities.

6. Review progress regularly.

7. Maintain accountability.

8. Reflect and assess.

Once you have your goals, **define the outcomes and impacts of your goals.** In other words, **write down what the successful completion of the goal will look like.** And also **write down the benefit of achieving the goal and how it relates to your values.** Writing down the benefits clarifies the reason for setting the goal in the first place, and it also serves as motivation later when you struggle to keep momentum in reaching the goal. If you lose momentum, review your written impacts and benefits to motivate yourself to achieve your goal.

As you define the benefit, answer a few of the following questions:

1. I will know I have completed this goal when I. . .

2. When I achieve this goal, I will benefit by. . .

3. Achieving this goal will allow me to. . .

4. Achieving this goal is important to me because. . .

Using the example goal of my book, following are my answers to these questions:

1. I will know I have completed this goal when I. . . actually publish the book!

2. When I achieve this goal, I will benefit by. . .feeling satisfied that I am being true to my values. I may make some money as well.

3. Achieving this goal will allow me to. . .have a positive impact on young people I may never meet. Writing the book will allow me to make a greater impact than I could without the book.

4. Achieving this goal is important to me because. . . the book should benefit the young people who read it. Plus, I have had the goal to write a book for several years; achieving this goal will be very fulfilling.

Next, define the major steps. **Your goal likely will require several steps.** Make an effort to define these steps and assign timeframes for completion. Understand that all the necessary steps may not be clear at first, and a little ambiguity is normal. I have worked with several gifted students who were motivated and goal-oriented and planned to work in a well-defined career. To achieve this goal, the students needed to go to graduate or law school. The problem was that the students did not know which law school or graduate school to attend. This lack of clarity was disheartening to some of the students because they thought they did not have a clearly defined path to their career goal. I encouraged the students to focus on what they did know and also to move forward with their next steps, which are specific tasks that need to be completed to move a project towards completion.

Although you may not have complete clarity in your next steps, you often have enough clarity to move forward. Don't underestimate the importance of knowing your next steps. Perhaps you have felt like you had a lot to do but did not know what to do next. This lack of direction can be paralyzing. By having a list of next steps for all your projects, you will know what to work on next. **My mentor taught me to always know the next two or three steps for everything on which I was working.** Following this advice greatly reduced wasted time as well as frustration because I always knew what to do next. Knowing your next steps requires that you spend time regularly planning and assessing your work, but this time is well spent.

Using the example of my book, following is a simplified list of next steps:

1. Develop an outline for chapters.

2. Develop an outline for subheadings.

3. Write the first draft.

4. Develop figures for each chapter.

5. Solicit input from students, pastors, teachers, advisors, early career professionals, and career counselors.

6. Revise text based on input from reviewers,

7. Select a publisher.

8. Submit the manuscript to the publisher.

Once you have developed a list of next steps, **get started**. Remember Proverbs 14:23: "In all labor there is profit, But mere talk leads only to poverty." If you want to profit from your goals, work on them. Be sure to **review your progress** regularly. If you have a goal that takes weeks or months to achieve, don't wait weeks or months to assess your progress. Periodically assess your progress, and ask yourself the following questions:

1. Am I on track with my plan?

2. What are my next steps?

3. Are there specific next steps that are behind schedule?

4. Has anything changed that will influence the priority of my goal?

5. Am I letting other things get in the way of this goal?

As you assess your progress, be especially mindful of priorities, time management, and context. It is easy to lose perspective of the value of the larger goal when you get mired down in the details and activities of the steps necessary to achieve the larger goal. **Review the benefits you wrote for your goals as you assess your progress.** The more you reinforce the beneficial impact of the goal you are working on, the better you will handle distractions and challenges that always accompany achievement of significant goals.

In addition to reviewing your progress, you will benefit from sharing your goals with someone (such as a mentor) who can keep you accountable. This person can check in with you to see if you are still progressing on your goals. **Sharing your** written goals with someone else and being accountable to that person will help you achieve your goals.

Finally, **once you achieve a goal, reflect on the goal itself and on the process of setting and achieving goals.** It's a good idea to celebrate your accomplishments and to reflect on what you learned about the process of setting and achieving goals. As you reflect, ask yourself the following questions and write your answers in your journal.

1. What worked well?

2. What didn't work well?

3. What have you learned that you can apply to your efforts to reach other goals?

Parable of the Garage Sale

Think back to when you were younger. Think about your favorite toy, the toy that you just had to have and that would give meaning to your life. Several toys were on my list, but one of the most coveted was a new sling shot. I envisioned myself slaying tin cans, skipping rocks across my grandfather's pond, and generally wreaking havoc in the woods. I finally got the slingshot, and it was nice...for a while. However, my sling shot soon ended up in a garage sale. What about the toy you really wanted? Where is it now?

The apostle Paul puts it this way: "7But whatever things were gain to me, those things I have counted as loss for the sake of Christ. 8More than that, I count all things to be loss in view of the surpassing value of knowing Christ Jesus my Lord, for whom I have suffered the loss of all things, and count them but rubbish so that I may gain Christ" (Philippians 3:7-8). Paul goes on to say: "13Brethren, I do not regard myself as having laid hold of *it* yet; but one thing *I do*: forgetting what *lies* behind and reaching forward to what *lies* ahead, [14]I press on toward the goal for the prize of the upward call of God in Christ Jesus" (Philippians 3:13-14).

You may really want something and spend tremendous amounts of time and effort striving for it only to relegate it to life's garage sale later on. **If you waste time pursuing things that only have a short-term impact or that do not align with your *true* God-given values, you lessen your ability to reach your true goals.** Furthermore, you likely will lack fulfillment. For example, several years ago I developed a great interest in photography. I spent a lot of time (and money) on it. Now, although I still enjoy photography, I realize that I spent too much time on it. Had I spent time on something more impactful, such as writing this book, I would have been better off in the long run.

The photography example illustrates the importance of being "future-oriented." The key point is that you should invest your time in activities that will benefit you in the future. Consider a high school student who wants to go to college. Rather than spending several hours on social media, the student should spend some time on future-oriented activities, such as the following:

1. Research potential universities to attend.

2. Visit the online career centers at several universities and go through their assessments to identify potential careers.

3. Review degrees offered at several universities and identify potential areas to major in.

4. Identify universities that you want to visit and determine how to schedule a campus tour.

Examples of future-oriented activities for college students include:

1. Search for summer internships or study-abroad opportunities.

2. Review online job descriptions to learn about education and experience requirements as well as the duties and responsibilities for careers you are interested in.

3. Review the website of the career center at your school. Be sure that you are utilizing the resources available to you.

List three future-oriented activities you can engage in:

1.

2.

3.

Key points from Chapter 9:

1. God's highest priority is that we love Him.

2. Values are those things that are important to you and should guide your overall direction in life.

3. Your values, goals, and priorities must align with God's plan for your life.

4. Goals are results or accomplishments that you want to achieve and should be aligned with your God-given values.

5. Priorities are those things that are important to you and that should preferentially receive your time and resources.

6. Don't waste your time shooting at the wrong target.

7. Write down your goals, including your benefits of achieving your goals.

8. Always know your next steps for all the projects you are working on.

9. Be future-oriented and spend time on activities that benefit your future and will have long-term impacts.

Please reflect on what you learned in this chapter and answer the following questions:

1. In your own words, explain what it means to know where you are going.

2. Why is it important to know where you are going?

3. What are the top two or three points that you learned from this chapter?

4. List three specific things you will work on for knowing where you are going.

5. What benefit will you experience by following through on the items listed in Question 4?

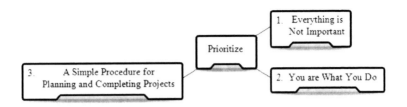

Chapter 10: Prioritize

Countless books have been written on prioritization and time management, yet my experience is that most people spend time doing things that are not a high priority. You may think you are making progress simply because you are busy. Nothing could be further from the truth. In fact, **busyness can keep you from accomplishing anything meaningful** by giving you a false feeling of accomplishment while stealing your time. Understanding this difference can have a huge impact on your success.

Recall that the apostle Paul emphasizes prioritization: "Therefore I run in such a way, as not without aim; I box in such a way, as not beating the air" (1 Corinthians 9:26). If you focus on priorities you will run with "aim" because you will run toward your goals. Your efforts will yield results, and you won't just waste time "beating the air." As a Christian you are called to pursue God as your highest priority, and you must prioritize His plan for your life. To do otherwise is simply a waste of time and energy.

Everything is Not Important

Manage your time so that you achieve your goals. Managing your time means that you **spend time on your priorities**, and it also means that you **do not waste time on non-priorities**.

The Bible gives an excellent example of the importance of focusing on your priorities rather than focusing on things of lower importance.

[38]Now as they were traveling along, He entered a village; and a woman named Martha welcomed Him into her home. [39]She had a sister called Mary, who was seated at the Lord's feet, listening to His word. [40]But Martha was distracted with all her preparations; and she came up *to Him* and said, "Lord, do You not care that my sister has left me to do all the serving alone? Then tell her to help me." [41]But the Lord answered and said to her, "Martha, Martha, you are worried and bothered about so many things; [42]but *only* one thing is necessary, for Mary has chosen the good part, which shall not be taken away from her (Luke 10:38–42).

Jesus visited the home of two sisters, Mary and Martha. Mary focused her attention on Jesus and His teaching of the Gospel. Martha, on the other hand, was busy doing other things around the house. She was upset that Mary was not helping and asked Jesus to tell Mary to help her. However, Jesus told Martha that spending time with Him is the highest priority. He went on to say that He would not "take away" the choice that Mary made. In essence, Jesus made the point that, even though the work Martha was doing was important, spending time with Him was the highest priority. You would be wise to **heed Jesus' example, and spend your time only on your highest priorities, which align with God's plan for your life.**

You can begin to identify your priorities by answering the questions below. Keep your priorities as simple and clear as possible.

Following are some questions to help you determine your priorities:

1. What is God's plan for your life?

2. What are your values?

3. What are your goals?

4.   What are your responsibilities?

5.   What is the impact of the activity?

The influence of God's plan, values, and goals on priorities was discussed earlier. Your responsibilities also influence your priorities. A student has the responsibility to attend class, complete assignments, learn the material, study for tests, and so on. An employee has the responsibility to go to work, contribute to teamwork, be self-motivated, and be productive. Your responsibilities to your family can have a tremendous effect on your priorities. Finally, as discussed in the Parable of the Garage Sale in Chapter 9, **your priorities should make an impact and have lasting value.**

Don't lose sight of your priorities when bombarded with other people's priorities. Someone may bring an issue to you seeking help; this issue may be a priority for him but not necessarily for you. By working on his priority, you lose time that could be spent on your priorities. Of course, his friendship may be a priority, so his issue may merit your time. Please understand that I am not discouraging you from helping others; in fact, helping others should be a priority. However, don't automatically place a higher priority on the requests of other people than on your own priorities. For example, if you have a major chemistry test in the morning but your roommate wants to tell you about his new motorcycle tonight, you would be wise to suggest to him that you talk about it tomorrow after your test. In other words, prioritize your need to study over his priority of talking about motorcycles.

Furthermore, understand that **urgent issues, whether yours or someone else's, are not necessarily important issues.** Many people struggle to recognize the difference between urgency and importance. I have observed this lack of understanding several times in interviews when I ask potential employees this question: "If you have urgent activities and important activities competing for your time, which would you work on first?" Many people incorrectly answer that they would first work on the urgent activities. The point is that the enthusiasm often associated with urgency counterfeits itself as importance. Don't be fooled: You should work on the most important things first, and remember that urgent issues are not necessarily important issues.

Once again, we see an excellent example in the Bible regarding the importance of focusing on your priorities rather than someone else's priorities. In this example, Mary and Martha's brother Lazarus is sick, and the sisters want Jesus to come right away and heal Lazarus.

> ³So the sisters sent word to Him, saying, "Lord, behold, he whom You love is sick." ⁴But when Jesus heard this, He said, "This sickness is not to end in death, but for the glory of God, so that the Son of God may be glorified by it." ⁵Now Jesus loved Martha and her sister and Lazarus. ⁶So when He heard that he was sick, He then stayed two days longer in the place where He was. ¹⁴So Jesus then said to them plainly, "Lazarus is dead, ¹⁵and I am glad for your sakes that I was not there, so that you may believe; but let us go to him." ⁴³When he had said this, Jesus called in a loud voice, "Lazarus, come out!" ⁴⁴The dead man came out, his hands and feet wrapped with strips of linen, and a cloth around his face.⁴⁵Therefore many of the Jews who came to Mary, and saw what He had done, believed in Him (John 11:3-6, 14-15, 43-45).

The Bible tells us that Jesus loved Mary, Martha, and Lazarus. Furthermore, we read in John 11:35 that "Jesus wept" for Lazarus. So it would seem that when Jesus heard the news of Lazarus' illness, He would go immediately to help. After all, this is a "life and death" situation. However, Jesus waited two days before He went. Why? Jesus waited because His priority was to draw people to Himself, ultimately leading to the salvation of sinners.

In other words, even though Jesus was informed of the life-and-death illness of His friend, Jesus stayed on His schedule and focused on His priorities. Jesus states in John 11:15 that: "I am glad for your sakes that I was not there, so that you may believe." When Jesus was ready, He and His disciples went to Lazarus, who was dead by this time. Jesus raised Lazarus from the dead, and "many" believed in Him.

Jesus was faced with an urgent priority of someone else, but He stuck with His priorities. His commitment to His priorities allowed Him to achieve His ultimate goal, giving salvation to sinners. Of course, Jesus often responded more quickly when others sought Him. When you are faced with the urgency of someone's request, pray to God for guidance; He will tell you how to respond.

You likely won't be summoned to resurrect anyone, so what might focusing on your priorities mean to you? Imagine you are trying to finish a class project that is due in the morning. As you are working, you get a text from your friend. The urgency of the text can interrupt your work, and you may get drawn into a conversation that should wait until after you finish your important project. If you spend a lot of time texting, you may not get your project done. Or you may hurry and poorly complete the project.

Of course, you want to respond to your friend's text, but likely you can wait until your important, priority work is done. You could text your friend and let her know that you will follow up after you get your work done. Avoiding the interruption is even better: Turn your phone off when you are working on something important. Small interruptions such as texts can decrease your efficiency.

You are What You Do

Once you separate the important from the urgent, **manage your time so that you can focus effort on your priorities.** In other words, spend your time working on your priorities so that you achieve your goals. Doing so is easier said than done. For several years, I taught an orientation class for college freshmen. I asked students to describe their biggest challenge. Without fail, year in and year out, the answer was the same: "I don't have enough time." Although it is true that you do not have time to do everything, you do have time to do what is truly important to you. Think of it like this: **The least effective person you know has the same amount of time as does the most effective person you know**. The difference, of course, is knowing how to manage your time, avoid distractions, and put maximum effort into your priorities. **Effective time management will have a huge impact on your success.** The apostle Paul encourages you to manage your time wisely: "[15]Therefore be careful how you walk, not as unwise men but as wise, [16]making the most of your time, because the days are evil. [17]So then do not be foolish, but understand what the will of the Lord is" (Ephesians 5:15-17).

If you spend time on non-priority activities, then obviously you have less time available for your priorities. Life is a series of choices. Choose wisely. **Saying "no" to some activities is as important as is saying "yes"**—perhaps even more so. A colleague of mine says, "When you say yes to something now, you are saying no to something else later." In the first Mary and Martha example, Martha said "yes" to her work, and thereby said "no" to spending time with Jesus. To reiterate this point, when asked if I have had time to do something I have not done, I often reply, "Yes, I had time. But I chose to spend my time on something else."

How do you know if you are managing your time effectively? Here are a few questions to consider:

1. Do you often think you could have done better on a task or project if you would have had more time?

2. Do you consistently miss deadlines?

3. Do you consistently ask for extra time to get your work done?

4. Do you have to pull "all-nighters" or rush at the last minute to get your work done?

If you answer "yes" to any of these questions, you should improve your time management skills. I will show you how to do so later in this chapter.

The importance of prioritization was driven home to me by a committee that evaluated the accomplishments I made during my first three years as an assistant professor. The committee provided recommendations to help me reach my goal of promotion and tenure. The recommendation was to quit doing some of the things I was doing and put more effort into the aspects of my job that would lead to promotion and tenure. In other words, prioritize.

Their advice, which sounds like common sense now, did not immediately resonate with me. I was working very hard, and I thought everything I was doing was important. And in some ways, everything I was doing was important. However, some activities would not help me reach my goal of achieving promotion and tenure. Thus, **although I was very busy and was working on several activities that seemed important, I was not spending enough time on activities that would help me reach my goal**. Achieving promotion and tenure was my top professional goal, and I should not have been investing time on activities that would not help me reach my goal. I was spending too much time on committees and not enough time on research. Were the committees important? Yes, but committee work would not contribute much to my promotion evaluation. To be promoted, I needed more research grant money and more publications.

Using the target example discussed earlier, my target (goal) was promotion and tenure, and spending time on committee work was shooting at the wrong target. Even though I was hitting the committee work target, time spent on committee work would not help me reach my goals. In other words, I was *doing things right*, but I was not *doing the right things*. Remember, being busy (doing something) is not the same thing as being productive (doing something important).

The difference between busyness and productivity can be difficult to see. Most people realize they are wasting time if they spend a lot of time online or playing video games. However, spending time on otherwise worthwhile activities can also get in the way of your progress if those activities are not your real priorities. Please don't miss this point: **Not all "important" activities are equal, and "good" activities can get in the way of your true priorities.**

For example, I often see young Christians busily doing "church stuff" rather than growing in their relationship with Jesus Christ. Involvement in church activities is important but does not substitute for your relationship with Jesus Christ. For example, many enthusiastic young Christians get involved in several outreach or service activities at church. Of course serving at your church is very important, and I encourage you to get involved. However, you also should spend time in prayer and reading your Bible. **Find the right balance so that you both grow in your relationship with Jesus Christ and serve your church.** Think of it like this: If you spend more taking care of the church lawn than you spend reading your Bible, you may be *mowing* but you are not *growing*!

Similarly, I often see college students spending too much time on student organization activities. Are these activities important? Absolutely. However, if they get in the way of your classes, they are getting in the way of a key priority for students: learning. I have seen the same problem with volunteerism. Although volunteerism is very important, it should be balanced with other priorities. Spending an entire weekend volunteering at the local animal shelter should not be your top priority if you have a major project due or have a test on Monday.

A Simple Procedure for Planning and Completing Projects

Let me end this section with a practical example of how I get organized, manage time, and stay focused on priorities. My approach may be helpful to you as well. When I start working on a project, I follow this procedure:

1.   Outline the steps that are needed.

2.   Estimate the time required for each step.

3.   Determine the deadline for each step.

4.   Add each step to my calendar.

5.   Stay focused on my plan to ensure I meet deadlines.

Following is an example of an outline you could use to write a term paper for school or a report for your job. Assume a deadline of February 15.

Step	Duration	Deadline
Outline the paper	1 hr.	Jan-15
Research your topic	4 hr.	Jan-20
Write first draft	2 hr.	Jan-22
Revise draft	1 hr.	Jan-25
Find someone to review your paper	—	Jan-26
Conduct additional research, if needed	2 hr.	Feb-3
Write second draft	2 hr.	Feb-6
Send second draft to reviewer	—	Feb-6
Write final draft	1hr	Feb-12
Submit		Feb-13

To begin, break down the project of writing a paper into steps. Estimate the time required to complete each step, and schedule your steps so you can finish your paper by the deadline. You might build in a one- or two-day cushion, in case you need extra time. Add this information to your calendar. (If you don't use a planning calendar, I suggest that you start using one.)

In this example, I estimated that outlining the paper would take an hour. The deadline was January 15. To complete this step, I block out an hour in my calendar to work on the outline, so I can finish it by the January 15 deadline. For example, I might set aside nine to ten a.m. on January 13 to work on the outline. I estimated that conducting research would take four hours. Thus, I block out two, two-hour time periods for my research. I may block out from ten a.m. to noon on January 17th, and from two p.m. to four p.m. on January 19th. Similarly, I block out time for each of the remaining steps. Think of blocking out time for your steps as setting up a meeting with yourself to ensure you have time to complete each step on time and stay on track. Make these time blocks and activities a priority, and do not miss the "meetings" with yourself.

Because I like to have someone read through drafts of my paper to help me find errors and areas that are not clear, I need to find a reviewer. Sending a quick e-mail to a friend to ask her to read my paper does not merit setting aside a block of time; I simply e-mail her before January 26, ask her if she could review my paper, and give her my deadlines for sending her the paper and for receiving her comments. Once I receive her comments, I can make the necessary changes and submit my paper on time.

If you stick with the plan you developed, you will get your paper done on time. Although you need not always be this formal, mentally working through this exercise is quite valuable. The key points are to:

1. Know what steps are needed to complete your project.

2. Know the amount of time required to complete each step.

3. Plan enough time to complete each step on time.

4. Schedule specific time into your calendar to allow you to complete each step.

5. Prioritize your time to get the work done according to your plan.

Let me end with time management advice I give to students: At the beginning of each semester, add to your calendar your class meeting times, work schedule, student organization meetings, and so on for the entire semester. Be sure to set aside time for Bible study and prayer. Then set aside time each week of the semester to complete your school work. You might schedule six or eight two-hour blocks each week. This will ensure that you always have time available each week to complete your school work. At the beginning of the semester you may not know exactly what you will have to work on during the eleventh week of the semester, but you will know that you have time scheduled to do it.

Key points from Chapter 10:

1. Spend your time on priorities aligned with God's plan for your life.

2. Busyness can keep you from accomplishing anything meaningful.

3. The least effective person you know has the same amount of time as does the most effective person you know.

4. Focus your efforts on your priorities.

5. Urgent issues, whether yours or someone else's, are not necessarily priority issues.

6. Not all important activities are equal, and good activities can get in the way of your true priorities.

7. Know what steps are needed to complete your project, and plan enough time to get the work done on time.

Please reflect on what you learned in this chapter and answer the following questions.

1. In your own words, explain what it means to prioritize.

2. Why is it important to prioritize?

3. What are the three most significant points you learned from this chapter?

4. List three specific things you will work on to prioritize.

5. What benefit will you experience by following through on the items listed in Question 4?

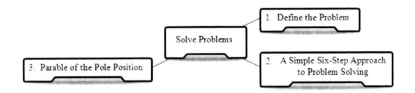

1. Define the Problem

Solve Problems

2. A Simple Six-Step Approach to Problem Solving

3. Parable of the Pole Position

Chapter 11: Solve Problems

Problem solving is a highly valued skill. **Successful people take the initiative to solve problems**. Perhaps you have heard that there are three kinds of people in the world: those who watch things happen, those who make things happen, and those who wonder what happened. Success most often goes to those who make things happen by solving problems.

Define the Problem

The most important step in solving a problem is defining the problem to the best of your ability. It has been said that if you can define a problem, you have it about fifty-percent solved. How do you define a problem? You think deeply about it and pray to God for wisdom and understanding to figure it out. James assures us that, "But if any of you lacks wisdom, let him ask of God, who gives to all generously and without reproach, and it will be given to him" (James 1:5). Similarly, King Solomon tells us: "For the Lord gives wisdom; From His mouth come knowledge and understanding" (Proverbs 2:6).

I learned the value of defining the problem while discussing with a colleague what I would work on as I started a new job. The conversation went something like this:

Me: "Enrollment in our college is a problem."
Him: "Well, what kind of a problem?"

Me:	"We don't have enough students."
Him:	"What's the problem?"
Me:	"We don't have enough students."
Him:	"Cary, what's the problem?"
Me;	"Well, our enrollment's not high enough."
Him:	"Cary, WHAT IS THE PROBLEM?"

After a few minutes, I realized that I was not answering his question. That conversation taught me a great lesson: Before you can solve a problem, you must define it. In this example, enrollment is influenced by several factors. To solve the enrollment problem, I first needed to understand which factors needed fixed.

It may seem obvious that you must define a problem before you solve it, but my experience is that people often hope to find a solution without necessarily knowing what the real problem is. I believe that King Solomon referred to this principle in Proverbs 18:13: "He who gives an answer before he hears, It is folly and shame to him." I referenced this verse in the garage door opener example and emphasized the importance of getting your facts straight before criticizing someone. In the context of problem solving, you don't want to try to solve the problem or "give an answer" before you "hear" what the real problem is.

Consider a car that won't start. You can change the battery or replace the starter, but if the problem is an empty gas tank, changing those parts will not help. Similarly, you certainly would not want to visit a doctor who gives you a shot in the backside without first figuring out why you are sick.

Consider the example of a student organization that has trouble getting students to attend meetings. How would you solve this problem? If you don't know why students are not showing up, you can't solve the problem very easily. The first thing to do is figure out why students don't attend. Perhaps students do not know when the meetings are. Maybe the meetings are boring, and nobody wants to come. Maybe the meetings are far from campus, and some students don't have cars. Perhaps the club meets at the same time as basketball practice, and many club members are on the basketball team.

Let's say that you have looked into the issue and found out that the basketball team does have practice at the same time as you have your meetings. You can change your meeting time, and attendance should increase.

Consider another scenario: What if attendance is low because the meetings are boring, and students don't gain anything from attending? Changing the meeting time won't change the fact that the meetings are boring. To increase attendance, change the meeting agenda to make your meetings more interesting and valuable to students.

Hopefully these simple examples illustrate the importance of defining the problem and understanding its core. **By asking several questions and defining the problem, you will know where to start looking for a solution.**

A Simple Six-Step Approach to Problem Solving

A quick Internet search of "problem solving" yields several different problem-solving approaches, ranging from four steps to more than ten. Following is a simple six-step process that can serve as a framework for you as you tackle problem solving:

1. Identify the problem.

2. Determine the underlying cause of the problem.

3. Determine possible solutions.

4. Select a solution.

5.   Implement the solution.

6.   Assess the solution.

In the example of the student meeting, the problem was identified as poor attendance (Step 1). Before solving the problem, however, we needed to determine the cause of poor attendance (Step 2). Next, we determined a few solutions (Step 3). One possible solution was to change the meeting time due to a conflict with basketball practice. Another possible solution was to change the meeting agenda so that members could benefit from the meetings.

In the first scenario, we chose to move the meeting time (Step 4) due to the conflict with basketball practice. By changing the meeting time (Step 5), we observed that attendance increased (Step 6) and that the problem was solved.

In the second scenario, we changed the meeting time (Step 5), but we determined that attendance did not increase (Step 6). We then looked more deeply and determined the meetings were boring (Step 2). To increase attendance, we need a better agenda (Step 3). We then improved the meeting agenda (Step 4 and 5), and observed that doing so solved the problem (Step 6.)

As you saw above, the first solution (changing the meeting time) may not solve the problem. Keep in mind that to solve problems, you must think creatively. To think creatively you must indeed *think*. Although this point seems obvious, people often get into a knee-jerk mode of doing things the way they always have. Sometimes, the approach is just to plow through and do things out of habit or try to solve problems using tools that worked earlier. There certainly is value in using experiences from the past to solve problems of the future. However, **think about what you are trying to do and ask the right questions rather than mindlessly plowing ahead.**

I developed a bonus question that teaches students in my introductory soil science class the importance of thinking through a problem: "Consider an Alfisol that contains 2.0% organic matter and has a fine sandy loam texture in the Ap horizon (surface 9 inches). How much soil is in a hole that is 7.25 cm deep, 0.25 m long, and 6 inches wide? State explicitly all assumptions." After several minutes of unit conversions, volume and density calculations, and head-scratching, students come up with a wide range of answers. Of course, the answer is "none" because there is no soil in a hole. Remarkably, few students actually arrive at that conclusion.

You don't have to be a soil scientist to answer this question. In fact, if you know nothing about soil science, you are more likely to solve this problem. To make this point to my students, I explain that most of them would have answered this question correctly prior to learning soil science; this concept certainly causes the students to re-evaluate what it means to learn. This exercise affords me the opportunity to teach (preach) about the importance of sorting through irrelevant information and actually understanding the problem to be solved, not to mention the need to use common sense. The point is you should not just dive into finding a solution without understanding the problem you are attempting to solve.

Parable of the Pole Position

By solving problems and producing results, you set yourself up for future resources and opportunities. Throughout my career, I have seen resources given to individuals, teams, or departments who were achieving great things and did not appear to need additional resources. I also have seen resources diverted away from individuals, teams, and departments who were less productive. Why would resources go to those who were already achieving as opposed to those who were not as productive? Why not invest in those entities that are behind and need the help?

Resources and opportunities often are given to those who have the greatest potential to achieve future results. If you have been productive in the past, you probably will be productive in the future. Thus, **the more successful you are, the more opportunities and resources will come your way**. If your grades are good, you are more likely to get a scholarship. If your work has been good, you are more likely to get a promotion. On the other hand, if you have not taken advantage of your opportunities or have not been very productive in the past, you may have a hard time convincing someone to invest in you.

The Bible illustrates this important principle in the "Parable of the Talents" in the Gospel of Mark. A full discussion of the parable is beyond the scope of this book, but I encourage you to read it. Here is a brief summary: A man entrusts to his workers different amounts of money (talents), either one, two, or five. He then goes on a trip. When he returns, he meets with his workers to see what they have done with the money he entrusted to them. The workers who received two or five talents doubled their money and were praised by the man. He gave them additional responsibility. The worker who received one talent did not make any more money. The man chastised the worker, and took away his money and give it the man who had ten talents. Jesus ends the parable by saying, "For to everyone who has, more shall be given, and he will have an abundance; but from the one who does not have, even what he does have shall be taken away" (Matthew 25:29).

The principle illustrated in this example is that God gives you abilities and opportunities, and if you use them wisely, He will bless you with greater resources and opportunities. Conversely, if you don't use what God has given you, it will be taken away and given to someone who is using his or her God-given "talent."

When working with students I also use the "Parable of the Pole Position" to make this point. Growing up in Indiana, I enjoyed watching the Indy 500. The race starts with thirty-three cars arranged in eleven rows, three cars across. The most advantageous position to be in at the start of the race is the pole position, the inside position of the first row. To determine who gets the pole position, drivers go through a series of time trials to see who has the fastest time; the fastest driver gets the pole position.

You might be tempted to think that the driver with the slowest speed should be put in the pole position to give that driver a chance. Or you might think that the fastest driver should be put in the back of the field because that driver can catch up. Although these philosophies may have merit in some aspects of life, success generally begets success; **those who achieve the most tend to get the most**.

At first glance, this concept seems like common sense; why even bother mentioning it in this book? I have included it here because I have seen countless young people miss this point. In fact, it took me a while to catch on to this concept when I was younger. Growing up, I had been used to getting things (good grades, favor from teachers, good breaks, opportunities, second chances, third chances, fourth chances, and so on) without much effort on my part. And that is OK when you are young. This is similar to taking the driver with the slowest time and moving him to the pole position (in other words, you get "moved up" without having to earn it). However, I have seen several young people mistakenly assume that opportunities and resources will continue to be handed to them as they progress to college and beyond. I also had this sense of entitlement when I was young. However, I soon learned that **the entitlement of my past did not match the realities of my present and future**. This contradiction took me by surprise. And I have seen many young people be surprised, frustrated, and disappointed as well.

If you want to be successful in the future, you have to earn it. The more you achieve, the more opportunities you will be given for further achievement. **Don't assume that success and opportunity will come your way just because they**

always have. If you want a scholarship, you have to work hard to get good grades. If you want a promotion at work, work hard and be very productive. If you assume success simply will be handed to you, you likely will find yourself frustrated as you watch others move ahead of you.

We discussed earlier that God's blessings will chase you down, and this is true. The words of the apostle Paul also are true, "Do you not know that those who run in a race all run, but only one receives the prize? Run in such a way that you may win" (1 Corinthians 9:24). As a Christian, God will send His blessings to chase you down, and He also will empower your success as you run to win.

Key points from Chapter 11:

1. Before starting to solve a problem, define the problem to the best of your ability.

2. God will give you wisdom to solve problems if you ask Him.

3. Follow the six-step problem-solving model.

4. Think creatively.

5. Use your God-given talents wisely, and God will reward you.

6. God will send His blessings to chase your down, and He also will empower your success as you run to win.

Please reflect on what you learned in this chapter and answer the following questions.

1. In your own words, explain what it means to solve problems.

2. Why is it important to solve problems?

3. What are the three most significant points you learned from this chapter?

4. List three specific things you will work on to solve problems.

5. What benefit will you experience by following through on the items listed in Question 4?

Chapter 12: Be Accountable

Successful people are accountable. Before we talk about what accountability is, let me illustrate what accountability is not. I once delegated responsibility to organize a youth retreat. My periodic check-ins led me to believe everything was on track. However, as the time for the retreat approached, I realized that the person I delegated to was not following through. When I approached the person to discuss the fact that the work was not getting done, I was given an excuse that is an excellent example of what accountability is not. The person said, "You should have known better than to put me in charge."

The Bible also contains a vivid example of what accountability is not. Adam and Eve lived in the Garden of Eden. God told them that they could eat anything they wanted in the Garden, except for the fruit of one particular tree. You may be aware that Eve gave into temptation and ate the fruit. She gave some fruit to Adam, and he at it as well.

When God confronted them and asked why they disobeyed, both Adam (the "man"), and Eve (the "woman") gave excuses instead of being accountable: "[12]The man said, 'The woman whom You gave to be with me, she gave me from the tree, and I ate.' [13]Then the Lord God said to the woman, 'What is this you have done?' And the woman said, 'The serpent deceived me, and I ate'" (Genesis 3:12-13). As you see, Adam blamed Eve and God, and Eve blamed the serpent.

These examples show that as long as people have lived on earth, we often have made excuses and dodged personal responsibility. As Christians, we ultimately are accountable to God, and we should be accountable for our work and for our mistakes.

Accountability Counts

Having just seen what accountability is not, what then is accountability? In the context of this book, accountability refers to personal responsibility. **When you are accountable, you take responsibility for your ability, behavior, attitude, and mistakes.** You should be true to, and accountable for, your own attitude, skills, and abilities and should strive to be the best you can be. To whom are you accountable? As a Christian, you are accountable to God, yourself, your parents, teachers, boss, and fellow Christians.

First and foremost, you are accountable to God. The apostle Paul tells us: "So then each one of us will give an account of himself to God" (Romans 14:12). A full discussion of Biblical accountability is beyond the scope of this book. The important point is that, for a person who dies without having accepted Jesus Christ as his or her Lord and Savior, accountability results in eternity in Hell. Conversely, as a Christian, your accountability focuses on rewards for what you have done with the opportunities that God has given you. Live your life according to God's plan, and you will receive God's rewards.

You also are accountable to yourself. If you compare yourself to others who have more natural ability or more experience than you have, you can get frustrated and think you can never accomplish what they do. This frustration can lead to a negative attitude, loss of confidence, and lack of desire to put forth the effort you otherwise would.

On the other hand, if you compare yourself to others who are less talented or less accomplished, you can get comfortable and never reach further to attain your potential. This concept is illustrated by the "Parable of the Leading Scorer." If the leading scorer on a team averages eighteen points per game, and the next-highest scorer averages ten points per game, the leading scorer may be satisfied and not try to improve. However, if the leading scorer has the ability to average twenty-five points per game, he is not reaching his true potential. By comparing himself to others, the leading scorer may not try to improve. You should be self-motivated to achieve your potential; this self-motivation requires God's strength, accountability, self-awareness, and a commitment to improve.

Accountability dictates that you take responsibility for your performance and not make excuses. I have talked to many students about a poor grade in a class, and the students said, "I didn't like the professor," or "That class was at eight a.m., and I am not a morning person." Frankly, none of that matters. You must take responsibility for your actions and for your own results. I also often hear, "I'm not good at math." Maybe you are; maybe you are not. But sometimes the "I'm not good at..." plea is just an excuse not to try.

I am guilty of the "I'm not good at ..." plea. I often say, "I'm not good at making repairs around the house." Actually, I have no desire to make repairs around the house. Whether or not I am good at making repairs is not the point. For me, it's an excuse not to try, and I think it is likely the same with others too.

Quality Matters

Accountability requires that you produce quality work. **Do your best work rather than just completing the work to check it off of your list.** I admit I have finished something just to say, "I finished it." Nearly every time I have taken this approach, it has backfired. The downside of this approach is that you may have to do the work again. Furthermore, people may start to associate you with sloppy work.

As Christians, we do our best because our lives should positively reflect Jesus Christ. The Bible contains several verses on the quality of our work, including the following:

- "Whatever you do, do your work heartily, as for the Lord rather than for men" (Colossians 3:23).
- "Whatever your hand finds to do, do it with all your might; for there is no activity or planning or knowledge or wisdom in Sheol where you are going" (Ecclesiastes 9:10).
- "With good will render service, as to the Lord, and not to men" (Ephesians 6:7).
- "Poor is he who works with a negligent hand, But the hand of the diligent makes rich" (Proverbs 10:4).
- "Whether, then, you eat or drink or whatever you do, do all to the glory of God" (1 Corinthians 10:31).
- "He also who is slack in his work is brother to him who destroys" (Proverbs 18:9)
- "Do you see a man skilled in his work? He will stand before kings; He will not stand before obscure men" (Proverbs 22:29).

These verses clearly show that God expects us to do our best work, because everything we do is "For the Lord." He also tells us that if we don't do our best work, we will be poor and we are similar to a destroyer. Conversely, God tells us that if we are skilled, we will "stand before kings." You can't be skilled if you don't do your best work. And you can't do your best work if you rely only on your own strength and ability. To truly do your best work, ask God to empower you and to demonstrate His power in and through your life.

My experience is that many young people frequently do less than their best work. As mentioned earlier, you have strengths in some areas, but not in all areas, and you cannot excel at every endeavor. However, **you should never be limited by your effort and never settle for doing less than your**

best. Frankly, I have been amazed by the number of students who simply won't put forth real effort. This is quite frustrating to me because I know that they could do better if they worked harder. I have seen several students whose GPAs reflected their effort rather than their ability. And I have seen these GPAs hold students back from getting into college, receiving scholarships, and securing internships and permanent jobs. On the other hand, I have seen some students with less natural ability greatly exceed the accomplishments of "smarter" students because of sheer effort. **Ask God to empower you to put forth your best effort.**

Furthermore, I have seen several cases in which a person puts forth his best effort on some activities, but not on all activities. This fact is commonly revealed to me when I review student evaluations provided by employers. The employers notice and clearly point out that a student does great when the student is working on something enjoyable, but that the quality of the work drops when the student is doing a task that is not enjoyable. I truly hope that God gives you a career in which you enjoy every task, and I hope that you enjoy every assignment in every class that you take. However, that likely won't happen.

To succeed in your career (or classes), put forth your best effort even when you are doing something you don't enjoy. Trust me on this one. I have seen enough in my classes and have received this feedback from enough employers to know that this problem is common. And I also know that employers are not interested in hiring people who only work hard on enjoyable tasks. More importantly, remember Paul's instructions to Christians: "Whatever you do, do your work heartily, as for the Lord rather than for men" (Colossians 3:23). Note that Paul says you are to work hard at "*Whatever* you do," not "Whatever you *like* to do."

Ensuring that your work meets the needs of those who will use it is another dimension of doing your best work. Consider the simple example of being asked for directions. If someone asks you for directions to your house, you could give her a map of the town you live in or you could give her turn-by-turn directions. The turn-by-turn approach is much better than just giving her a map. The map could work, but she would have to spend a lot of time trying to figure out how to get to your house.

When you are asked to complete a task for someone, think about how you can best meet the needs of the person making the request. My experience is that many people do the minimum amount of work necessary to finish a task without considering the needs of the end user; this lack of consideration demonstrates poor accountability. **Always do your work so that your final product meets the needs of the person who will use it.** This is the same concept discussed in Chapter 5 where I emphasized the importance of focusing on your audience rather than on yourself when communicating and going the extra mile.

Consider an example where you are to find a hotel for a leadership retreat for a student organization. One approach is to find a list of all the hotels in the town where the retreat will be held, and report back with this simple list. However, a better approach is to check with the hotels to determine costs, availability of rooms, and extras such as free WIFI or breakfast. You can then report back with meaningful information rather than just a simple list.

Consider another example of your boss asking you for five years of sales data from three competitor companies. You could provide your boss a link to the websites of each company so she could look up the information. Or, you could give her copies of the annual reports from the companies so that she can find the information. From one perspective, you provided the information your boss wanted (and can check it off of your list). However, this approach represents a minimal amount of effort. A better approach is to find the sales data and summarize it in a form the boss can use without having to spend time combing through reports and websites. Although this extra effort may seem obvious to some, my experience is that many people will do the minimum to get by. **Set a goal to exceed expectations when asked to complete a task, and you will be surprised at the positive effect this has on your relationships, reputation, and your success.**

Before we leave our discussion of exceeding expectations, let me point out how this approach can benefit you greatly. I am often requested to write reference letters for students seeking jobs, awards, scholarships or admittance into law school, veterinary school, or graduate school. I write the strongest letters for those students who exceeded my expectations. I will provide in my letter details of how the student went above what was required. Such examples often are the key to receiving an award or scholarship, or gaining admittance into a program. Think of it this way: Nearly all of the students who apply for these awards and programs are excellent students with excellent records of leadership and involvement. **The students who stand out as exceptional are those who have gone above and beyond what is expected.** Furthermore, you are a better ambassador for Jesus Christ when you exceed the expectations.

Handling Mistakes

You must be accountable for your mistakes. No one likes mistakes, but nearly everyone makes mistakes. No one likes excuses, but many people make excuses when they make mistakes. No one respects people who use excuses instead of accountability. I have worked with people who were gifted at making excuses and greatly lacking in accountability. That behavior is rancid on teams and in the workplace. Furthermore, rarely is anyone fooled for very long by the excuses.

When your mistakes are sins, confess to God and ask Him to forgive you. The apostle John assures us that: "⁹If we confess our sins, He is faithful and righteous to forgive us our sins and to cleanse us from all unrighteousness" (1 John 1:9). Furthermore, King David says: "As far as the east is from the west, So far has He removed our transgressions from us" (Psalm 103:12).

Although God will forgive you and remove your transgressions, consequences remain. If you confess to God that you cheated on a test, He will forgive you. But, you may receive an F on the test. Still, God in His grace can cause everything to work together for good (Romans 8:28.) Recall that Jonah disobeyed God's instruction to go to Nineveh, and he suffered the consequences of his sinful disobedience. God gave Jonah a second chance (Jonah 3:1), and He can give you another chance as well.

The Bible contains several verses discussing handling and recovering from your sinful mistakes, including the following:

- "He who conceals his transgressions will not prosper, But he who confesses and forsakes them will find compassion" (Proverbs 28:13).
- "When he falls, he will not be hurled headlong, Because the Lord is the One who holds his hand" (Psalm 37:24).
- "'I acknowledged my sin to You, And my iniquity I did not hide; I said, 'I will confess my transgressions to the LORD'; And You forgave the guilt of my sin. Selah.'" (Psalm 32:5).
- "Therefore there is now no condemnation for those who are in Christ Jesus" (Romans 8:1).
- "Therefore let us draw near with confidence to the throne of grace, so that we may receive mercy and find grace to help in time of need" (Hebrews 4:16).
- "For a righteous man falls seven times, and rises again, But the wicked stumble in time of calamity" (Proverbs 24:16).
- "The Lord sustains all who fall And raises up all who are bowed down" (Psalm 145:14).
- "And we know that God causes all things to work together for good to those who love God, to those

who are called according to His purpose" (Romans 8:28).

Note that if you admit your mistakes and don't make the mistake again, you will find compassion. God's grace removes your guilt and its burden on you. Notice also that several verses show that God will help you when you make mistakes. In fact, you can come with confidence to God and receive mercy and grace. Finally, notice that God causes all things to work for good, if you live your life according to His plan for your life.

Following is a list of helpful steps to take when you make a mistake:

1. Recognize you made a mistake.

2. Take responsibility for it.

3. Apologize for it.

4. Fix it if you can.

5. Take the necessary steps to ensure it does not happen again (learn from it.)

6. Move ahead.

Do not try to hide or cover up a mistake. You will look foolish when it is discovered. Once you recognize your mistake, admit it and take responsibility for it. Next, apologize. Never underestimate the importance of good common courtesy. Sometimes sincerely saying you're sorry is the best and only thing you can do. After you apologize, fix the problem if you can.

Looking forward, take measures to ensure that the mistake does not happen again. People usually will be patient with you when you make a mistake if you apologize, own up to it, and fix it. However, you must learn from your mistake and not make it again.

Finally, after you've recognized it, taken responsibility for it, apologized for it, fixed it, and made sure it won't happen again, move on. Don't play it over and over again in your mind. Sometimes I will make a mistake, and I will bash myself over it for long periods of time. That is a curse of perfectionism.

As long as we're on the subject of mistakes, keep in mind that successful people often make mistakes. At first, this fact may not make sense because you may think that you can't succeed if you make mistakes. However, mistakes in this context are made by people who step up to challenges and take risks. **Successful people take risks and thus make mistakes and experience failure.** The key is to learn from your mistakes and move past them. You can overcome mistakes if you learn from them and move ahead.

The point is you need to take calculated risks (not reckless, irresponsible, or dangerous risks). If you're working on a project and you're not exactly sure what to do, ask God for guidance. Then, trust God and move ahead in faith. Remember to be "strong and courageous!" **Roll out your ideas in small steps and continually assess progress.** If you find you're going in the wrong direction, stop, pray for clarity, make adjustments, and move ahead.

Furthermore, understand that God will allow you to make mistakes. You might make a mistake by getting outside of God's plan for your life. Or perhaps God needs to teach you something that you can learn only through a mistake. Recall that God taught me through our "futility treatments" experience to pray more genuinely and truly seek His will. Indeed, we often learn more from our mistakes than from our successes. **When you make a mistake, ask God what He wants you learn, do what He tells you to do, and remember the words of the apostle Paul: "And we know that God causes all things to work together for good to those who love God, to those who are called according to His purpose"** (Romans 8:28).

Understand that I'm not glorifying mistakes. When you make a mistake in judgment or in ethics, you may not get a second chance. I know of a very tragic case of a young person who tried drugs once; that one time cost him his life. Mistakes are going to happen, though, and the best thing to do is own up to them and learn from them.

Key points from Chapter 12:

1.   Everyone is accountable to God.

2.   Set a goal to exceed expectations.

3.   Always put forth maximum effort and rely on God's strength.

4.   Be accountable for your mistakes.

5.   Be willing to take calculated risks.

6.   God can use your mistakes to teach you what you need to know.

Please reflect on what you learned in this chapter and answer the following questions:

1.   In your own words, explain what it means to be accountable.

2.   Why is it important to be accountable?

3.   What are the three most significant points you learned from this section?

4.   List three specific things you will work on to be more accountable.

5.   What benefit will you experience by following through on the items listed in Question 4?

Summary and Concluding Thoughts

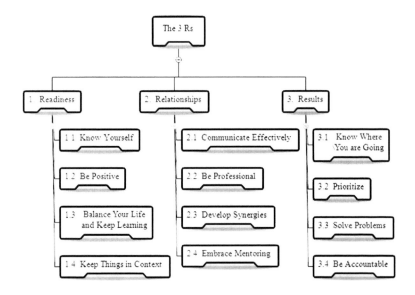

Your success is the ultimate goal of this book. True success requires you to live according to God's plan, to accomplish what He calls you to do, and to receive the blessings He has for you. To achieve success, you must trust God to work in and through your life and you must develop your leadership and soft skills.

I describe three key steps for developing your leadership and soft skills as knowing what you need to know, developing the abilities and behaviors you need, and having an attitude of achievement. To allow you to work through these three steps, and to achieve these goals, I present the 3 Rs: *Readiness*, *Relationships*, and *Results*.

The first R, *Readiness*, has at its core self-awareness and the need to truly understand yourself. If you are committed to developing your leadership and soft skills you must know yourself and recognize and maximize your God-given strengths as well as recognize and allow God to demonstrate His strength in your weaknesses. *Readiness* requires faith in God, and a positive attitude to provide buoyancy and endurance as you encounter inevitable challenges and trials in your life. *Readiness* requires commitment to lifelong learning and life balance. If you don't continue to learn and grow, or if your life lacks balance, you likely will fall short of achieving as much in life as you otherwise could. Finally, *Readiness* mandates that you maintain the proper context to see the greater perspective of your God-given values, goals, and priorities. If you lose sight of God's plan for your life, you will flounder in your daily routine, and fail to experience God's best blessings. Keep your setbacks in proper context. Focusing on setbacks will rob you of the desire to move ahead. Instead, keep your eye focused on what you want to achieve, bounce back from your inevitable setbacks, and move ahead.

The second R, *Relationships*, has at its core communication and professionalism. Effective communication is absolutely critical to your ability to build personal and professional relationships that will serve as the foundation for your personal and professional fulfillment. Creating and maintaining relationships requires professionalism and the ability to leverage the abilities of others. Put aside biases and work with a wide variety of people in your school, community, and workplace. Your relationship with Jesus Christ is your top priority. Developing a mentoring relationship with a mature Christian will enhance your faith and your professional development.

The third R, *Results*, has at its core future orientation and knowledge of where you are going. Develop clearly defined goals that are anchored to your God-given values, and prioritize your efforts to achieve these goals. Focus on results, put forth your best effort, and ask God to empower you to accomplish all He has planned for you. Finally, be accountable, and focus on problem solving to positively impact your family, school, community, workplace, and world.

I expect that this book gives you the tools and encouragement you need, and I trust that you are committed to continuing your success journey. I expect that you will follow God's plan for your life and rely on His strength to empower you. Please keep in mind there is no silver bullet for this journey. Think of your journey as a synergistic collection of many smaller steps instead of as a single big step. And realize that even small steps will move you forward. Celebrate your progress along the way, no matter how small it may appear.

As you develop your leadership and soft skills, please note that **you don't have to improve everything at once**. Development is a process; **don't expect perfection, but strive for continual progress.** Focusing on a few developmental goals and making real progress is better than having many goals that are never reached.

As suggested at the beginning of the book, study the scriptural references and review your notes and key points of each chapter. Read again the material that may not be clear. Also, please note that as you read through this again, you likely will discover points that you missed the first time you read the book. Ask God to show you areas to review.

Finally, truly believe that God wants you to succeed and that He will empower your success. Trust God and be willing to challenge yourself. Remember that if everything you attempt is easy for you, your goals are too small. **Dare to trust God, set big goals based on His plan for your life, put aside your doubts, and move ahead.**

Frankly, this book is an excellent example of what can happen if you trust God, set a big goal, and put forth real effort. I have wanted to write this book for years, but I had doubts. I was not sure I could write something that young people would want to read. However, because the goal of writing the book was anchored to my God-given values and because God gave me relevant skills and abilities, I determined that I would put my best effort into writing this book. I prayed fervently, sought God's guidance, and believed He called me to write this book. The fact that you are reading it is testimony that God's goals for your life can be accomplished. If you put aside your doubts, pursue your God-given goals, and put forth real effort, you can achieve what God calls you to achieve.

My expectation is that you will do what I have done. Seek God's guidance, set big goals aligned with God's plan, commit yourself to your goals, and trust God to empower you to make them happen. Then, like Paul, you can say: "I have fought the good fight, I have finished the course, I have kept the faith" (2 Timothy 4:7).

Thanks for reading my book. For additional resources and information on my personalized coaching program, please visit my website site (www.Leadershipandsoftskills.com) and Facebook page (www.facebook.com\leadershipandsoftskills). You can also follow me on Twitter (@EmpChristians). I invite you to send me your questions and comments. I am especially interested to know how this book has helped you grow as a Christian. I look forward to hearing from you.

Blessings to you.

Cary J. Green, PhD

CPSIA information can be obtained at www.ICGtesting.com
Printed in the USA
LVOW10s1716060416

482460LV00007B/56/P

9 781457 540998